STREET OF DREAMS®

LUXURY HOME PLANS

SHOW 50 HOMES

HOME PLANNERS
TUCSON, ARIZONA

D1609555

HOME PLANNERS, LLC
Wholly owned by
Hanley-Wood, LLC

John Shaheen / *Architectural Director*
Laura Hurst Brown / *Editor*
Paul Fitzgerald / *Senior Graphic Designer*

Jennifer Skiffington / *Editorial Assistant / Text*
Jeanine Newsom / *New Products Editor*
Alan Mitchell / *Plans Editor / Text*
Matthew S. Kauffman / *Graphic Designer*
Robert D. Caldwell / *Graphic Production Artist*
Fariba Crawford / *Manufacturing Assistant*
Victoria M. Frank / *Supervisor / Data Acquisition*
Brenda McClary / *Publications Assistant*

Cindy Coatsworth Lewis / *Director of Publishing*
Jan Prideaux / *Executive Editor*
Paulette Mulvin / *Special Projects &*
 Acquisitions Editor
Marian E. Haggard / *Associate Editor / Specialist*
Arlen Feldwick-Jones / *Associate Editor*
Sarah Smith / *Associate Editor*
Morenci Wodraska / *Plans Editor*
Kristin Schneidler / *Plans Editor*
Gerry Mallonee / *New Products Editor*
Sara Lisa / *Manufacturing Coordinator*
Jay C. Walsh / *Mac Systems Administrator*
Chester E. Hawkins / *Graphic Designer*
Peter Zullo / *Graphic Production Artist*
Joan C. Watson / *Data Acquisition Specialist*
Chuck Tripp / *Director of Retail Sales*
Hugh Shiebler / *National Key Account Manager*

Stephen Williams / *Publisher*
Rickard D. Bailey / *CEO & President*

Hanley-Wood, LLC:
Michael M. Wood / *Chief Executive Officer*
Frank Anton / *President*
John M. Brannigan / *Senior Vice President /*
 Corporate Sales Director
James D. Zielinski / *Chief Financial Officer*
Paul Kitzke / *Vice President /*
 Corporate Editorial Director
Ann Seltz / *Vice President / Marketing*
Maxx MacConnachie / *Vice President / Circulation*
Joanne Harap / *Vice President / Production*
Janice Bigelow / *Vice President / Finance*
Adriaan Bouten
 Vice President / Information Technology
Leslie S. Elsner
 Vice President / Human Resources

Editorial and Corporate Offices:
3275 West Ina Road, Suite 110
Tucson, Arizona 85741

Distribution Center:
29333 Lorie Lane, Wixom, MI 48393

Street of Dreams® photography by
getdecorating.com
email: info@getdecorating.com
or call toll-free 1-800-670-7500

Home Planners wishes to acknowledge the help of
Mr. David P. Straughan and Mr. M. Bryan Ashbaugh
with this publication.

First printing, February 2000
10 9 8 7 6 5 4 3 2 1

Library of Congress CCN: 00 130057
ISBN 1-881955-60-5

CONTENTS

65

139

80

138

213

from the editor

grand groundbreakers

Welcome to a dazzling celebration of today's hottest trends in residential architecture. Flowing curves, bold straight lines, simple horizontals and chic verve set off these stunning show homes. Each design displays a singular character created by the once-only gathering of a designer, builder and architect who together develop a fully unique and wholly comfortable dream home.

For over a decade, the exceptional quality of luxury home tours by Street of Dreams, Inc. has raised the bar on excellence in the world of residential design. Of course, raising dreams from the ground up is also what Home Planners is all about—and we've been at it for more than 50 years. Our vision of what home can be starts with the owner's most intimate notion of space and ends with an eye-catching residence unlike any other. We're pleased to present this full-color collection of premier custom homes as a welcome, first-ever collaboration of Street of Dreams, Home Planners and the designers and builders they represent.

This extraordinary portfolio of plans includes the brightest and best of the Street of Dreams® tours plus a diverse mix of fully furnished custom homes selected from the most captivating and cutting-edge neighborhoods in North America. Both sophisticated and practical, these styles represent an uncommon expression of taste and elegance. Best of all, construction drawings are available for each of these plans, so if you're in the market for a luxury home, these glamorous pages may beckon you to do more than just browse—you may decide to build the house of tomorrow today.

Laura Hurst Brown
Editor

ON THE COVER
DESIGNER: MCDOWELL & ASSOCIATES, INC.
BUILDER: LARATTA HOMES
INTERIOR DESIGN: SALLY HEALY DESIGN LTD.
PHOTOGRAPH: VISUAL SOLUTIONS CO.
TITLE PAGE: VISUAL SOLUTIONS CO.

Visit our website at www.homeplanners.com

ESTATE AT TRINITY BEND

DESIGN BY FRED PARKER COMPANY, INC.

Modern Classic

Rich in detail and lavish amenities, this elegant European Renaissance home of classic red brick is designed for 21st-Century living.

The majesty of the Estate at Trinity Bend comes from a unique blend of rumbled red brick and cast-stone enhancements with a stately interior rich with historic details. From the covered front porch, double French doors open to a grand entry foyer with twin spiral, floating stairways and an elaborate ironwork banister with inlaid paneling. The barrel-vaulted hall ceiling houses a bronze and crystal chandelier that casts a warm glow on the surrounding wood and marble. Throughout the home, custom-designed wood mantels and carvings complement rich warm colors such as delft blue, persimmon red and butter cream yellow for a friendly and elegant tone.

STREET OF DREAMS

Estate at Trinity Bend

Rich butter cream yellow walls warm the formal dining room.

*Elaborate ironwork, marble
floors and twin spiral, floating
stairways create a grand
entry.*

Parker Designs and The Design Studio of Gabberts designed the interior to reflect
a sense of elegant living. Past the foyer, the two-story grand room boasts a
twenty-three foot ceiling, enhanced by two overhanging balconies—one serving
as a library and the other a gallery to showcase art. A curved wall of windows
overlooks the rear gardens, which boast an exquisite nature pool, a natural rock
stream with waterfall, and a putting and chipping green. A massive fireplace
framed by built-in bookshelves enhances the stunning view.

To the left of the entry, the formal dining room features a brick and Rumford Old World fireplace and embossed ceilings. A sizable butler's pantry leads to the gourmet kitchen, which has its own walk-in pantry. The climate-controlled wine cellar facilitates the entertainment of guests. State-of-the-art appliances adorn the open-concept commercial kitchen, designed to accommodate planned events as well as family meals.

To the rear of the plan, the family room leads to the kitchen through an arched pass-through, and provides a fireplace, access to the rear patio, and a separate staircase to the sec-

This home, as shown in the photographs, may differ from the actual blueprints. For more detailed information, please check the floor plans carefully.

The executive study features oak woodwork and designer wall coverings.

Two-story windows allow splendid views in the grand room.

Opposite: A gourmet kitchen serves a snack counter and overlooks the spacious yet comfortable family room.

Tall windows and a fireplace both warm and define the game room—a tranquil retreat for a quiet read.

ond floor. A guest bedroom with private bath is also on this side of the home.

An executive study just off the foyer can easily be used as a parlor or home office but also serves the owners suite as a reading room. With built-in oak bookcases and detailed oak wainscoting, the study provides a private bath and a separate entrance to the exercise room and master suite.

The octagon-shaped owners suite has a vaulted beam ceiling, fireplace, lavish bath and private courtyard with a waterfall fountain, collecting pool and rock wall. The owners bath features a coffee bar, space for a TV behind the mirror, a whirlpool tub, separate shower, wardrobe room and dedicated exercise room.

Upstairs, via the stairs or the elevator, two bedrooms, each with private bath and walk-in closet, provide room for family or guests. Across the bridge, the English gentleman's clubroom features a traditional game table and wet bar. The home theater is fully equipped with surround sound and is near a convenient powder room. The hobby room leads to attic storage and outdoors to a balcony that overlooks the rear gardens.

On the third floor, a studio provides space for an additional bedroom with a private bath, wet bar and balcony. Luggage closets flank the room. Downstairs, the utility room has plenty of counter and work space, including its own island and sink.

DESIGNER: © Fred Parker Company, Inc., Fort Worth, Texas
BUILDER: Fred Parker Design Group
INTERIOR DESIGN: Parker Designs and The Design Studio of Gabberts
PHOTOGRAPHS: © Visual Solutions Co.

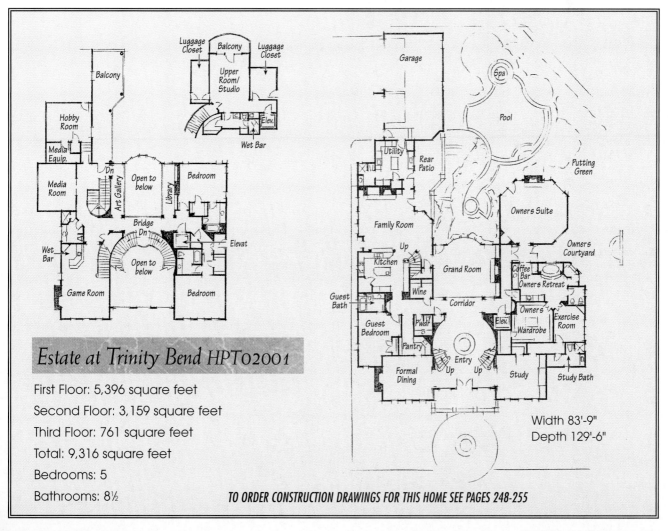

Estate at Trinity Bend HPT02001

First Floor: 5,396 square feet

Second Floor: 3,159 square feet

Third Floor: 761 square feet

Total: 9,316 square feet

Bedrooms: 5

Bathrooms: 8½

Width 83'-9"
Depth 129'-6"

TO ORDER CONSTRUCTION DRAWINGS FOR THIS HOME SEE PAGES 248-255

A finely crafted balustrade sets a modern yet elegant tone for the foyer.

MAPLE GLENN

DESIGN BY STEPHEN FULLER, AMERICAN HOME GALLERY

Classic Balance

Traditional design elements and an open free-flowing floor plan come together in a graceful home.

Stately brick and finely crafted front and rear porches complement an aesthetic symmetry of shutters, triple dormers and soaring, massive chimneys on this American Classic home. A portico supported by round columns enhances the stately façade. French doors topped by a fanlight window open to the foyer, which has a checkerboard-tiled floor. Columns subtly define the spaces of the living room to the left and the dining room to the right, each with a fireplace and two large windows overlooking the front yard.

Triple dormers, soaring twin chimneys and a portico supported by round columns to create a stately façade.

STREET OF DREAMS
Maple Glenn

A fireplace warms the formal living room, creating a space that's well suited for planned occasions and cozy gatherings.

Opposite: A walkout basement could provide added living space.

The formal dining room enjoys a fireplace and two large windows overlooking the front yard.

The foyer leads past an archway to the great room—a thoughtful mix of elegance and practicality, with built-in bookshelves, a vaulted ceiling and French doors to the covered rear porch. The great room shares a through-fireplace with the owners suite, which occupies an entire wing of the home. A private vestibule has a luxurious bath that includes a garden tub, an angled shower and separate vanities. Two walk-in closets and a French door that opens to the rear porch complete the retreat.

On the opposite side of the first floor, the kitchen easily serves planned events as well as casual meals. A center island and a walk-in pantry add convenience, and the kitchen opens to a bright breakfast room. The formal dining room provides a privacy door, which allows quiet conversation. The breakfast room leads to a side porch, perfect for warm-weather dining or access to the two-car garage. Nearby, a laundry room provides additional counter and cabinet space.

Throughout the first floor, details such as hardwood floors and carved molding help to create a timeless style, which continues on the second floor. A balcony hall overlooking the great room and stair hall links the three secondary bedrooms, each with a walk-in closet.

DESIGNER: © Stephen Fuller,
American Home Gallery
PHOTOGRAPHS: © Dave Dawson Photography

This home, as shown in the photographs, may differ from the actual blueprints. For more detailed information, please check the floor plans carefully.

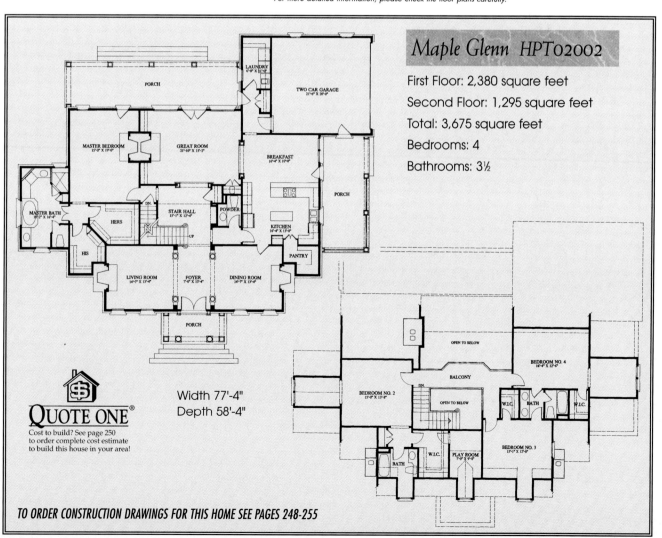

Maple Glenn HPT02002

First Floor: 2,380 square feet

Second Floor: 1,295 square feet

Total: 3,675 square feet

Bedrooms: 4

Bathrooms: 3½

Quote One®

Cost to build? See page 250 to order complete cost estimate to build this house in your area!

Width 77'-4"
Depth 58'-4"

TO ORDER CONSTRUCTION DRAWINGS FOR THIS HOME SEE PAGES 248-255

ARUNDEL MANOR

DESIGN BY HOME PLANNERS

Sweet Georgian

A spectacular classic takes its cues from Tulip Hill, an 18th-Century manor in Arundel County, Maryland.

This dignified brick home features the symmetrical façade and classical details of the Georgian era. The two-story center section perfectly complements the 1½-story wings—a primary feature of the style. A round window tops the pediment and complements the graceful portico. Past the box-paneled door, a two-story foyer opens to the formal rooms and features a stunning staircase. An elegant brass chandelier illuminates the area, enhanced by natural light from the window and transom above the door.

To the left of the entrance, the study features a massive fireplace and hand-built oak paneling. Its natural beauty combined with the fine oak trim and handcrafted oak

Stately and sophisticated, this Georgian home has a heart of gold.

This home, as shown in the photographs, may differ from the actual blueprints.
For more detailed information, please check the floor plans carefully.

Fanlights above multi-pane windows admit a generous portion of natural light.

grilles shames today's casual standards. On the opposite side of the foyer, the formal dining room provides its own fireplace and views of the front property. An ornate wood mantel provides a focal point, while two windows, each with a fanlight, illuminate the room. A crystal chandelier, suspended from a center-ceiling medallion, lends its own special light. Nearby, a thoughtfully placed powder room is convenient for guests.

Three steps down from the study or library is the great room—a perfect place to entertain in a grand fashion. The modified model has an expansive paneled wall that includes a media center built by hand. Opposite this wall, a large brick fireplace is topped with a simple, yet refined wood mantel. Five windows, each with an intricately detailed fanlight, allow plenty of sunlight to fill the room. Soaring, twelve-foot ceilings add dimension and enhance the room's atmosphere, while maintaining an air of formality. Two sliding glass doors provide access to the rear wood deck.

A well-organized kitchen is the real heart of this home. A center island dominates the area and can be used as a food preparation site or a serving table for buffets, with the

cooktop located here or on one of the countertops. The adjoining breakfast nook provides a sliding glass door that leads to the deck.

Upstairs, the owners suite offers an open and airy atmosphere with plenty of space to kick off your shoes and relax. French doors open to a refined bath, which includes a raised whirlpool tub set in a tiled platform and illuminated by a window. A magnificent sunken lounge, secluded behind the suite, provides a private haven. A fireplace or built-in entertainment center may easily be added to this room. Three additional bedrooms share a full bath.

DESIGNER: © Home Planners
PHOTOGRAPHS: © Laszlo Regos

An efficient island kitchen with an adjacent breakfast nook easily serves family and guests.

Stunning handcrafted details enhance every corner of this magnificent plan.

Oak paneling and a planked floor are the right touches to reflect the glow of a cozy fire in the first-floor study.

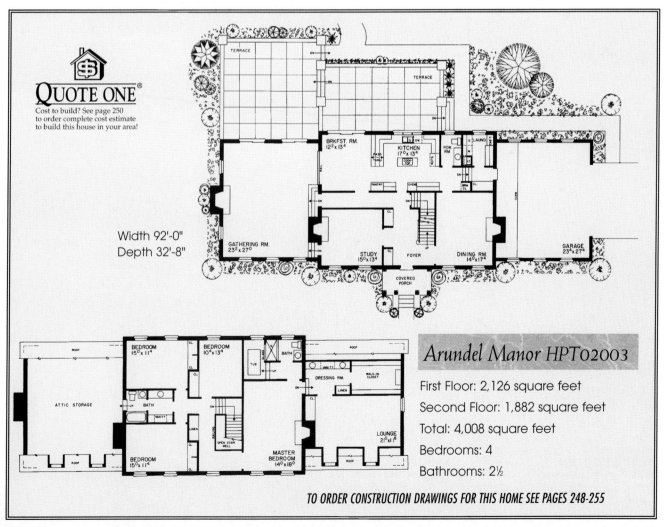

Width 92'-0"
Depth 32'-8"

Arundel Manor HPT02003

First Floor: 2,126 square feet

Second Floor: 1,882 square feet

Total: 4,008 square feet

Bedrooms: 4

Bathrooms: 2½

TO ORDER CONSTRUCTION DRAWINGS FOR THIS HOME SEE PAGES 248-255

*A sweeping double stairway highlights
an elegant receiving hall.*

KENTLANDS ESTATE

DESIGN BY HOME PLANNERS

Grand Reception

The elegance of traditional Georgian design is revived in this gracious home—and brought together with ultra-comfortable amenities.

This classic Georgian design includes a variety of features that make it an outstanding home: a pediment gable with cornice work and details, beautifully proportioned columns and classic window treatments. Four stately columns support a large pediment that provides shelter for the entry and announces a special interior designed to spoil the homeowner. Beyond the double doors, the majestic two-story foyer features twin curving stairways, topped by exquisitely crafted wood railings. An elegant brass chandelier and tall windows illuminate the receiving hall and present a warm welcome to all that enter.

Quoins accent the stately brick façade of this Colonial-style home.

The spacious owners suite provides a fireplace and a sitting area.

Opposite: The view from the rear of the plan is as spectacular as from the front.

A fireplace flanked by bookcases is the focal point for this comfortable living room.

The foyer opens on either side to the formal dining and living rooms. The spacious living room includes a fireplace and the dining room has built-ins appropriate for displaying fine china. The foyer also leads to the rear of the home and the massive gathering room. The family will spend many pleasurable hours in this room, made cozy by a centered fireplace. Built-in bookshelves, a must-have for the literature buff, adorn the walls on either side of the fireplace. A spacious study is located between the gathering and living rooms. This room, perfect for a home office, includes access to the rear terrace.

This home, as shown in the photographs, may differ from the actual blueprints. For more detailed information, please check the floor plans carefully.

Informal living revolves around the breakfast room and kitchen, which features a center cooktop island with plenty of storage. The second floor includes the owners suite, which provides over 360 square feet of living space—more than enough room for a sitting area and entertainment center, in addition to sleeping space. French doors open to a large deck—a perfect place to enjoy fresh breezes. The owners retreat also provides an angled corner tub, a separate shower, dual vanities and a walk-in closet. The right side of the plan holds two family bedrooms that share a full bath. The fourth bedroom, ideal for a guest suite, has its own bath. The family fleet of vehicles will enjoy the shelter and space of a three-car garage.

DESIGNER: © Home Planners
PHOTOGRAPHS: © Andrew D. Lautman

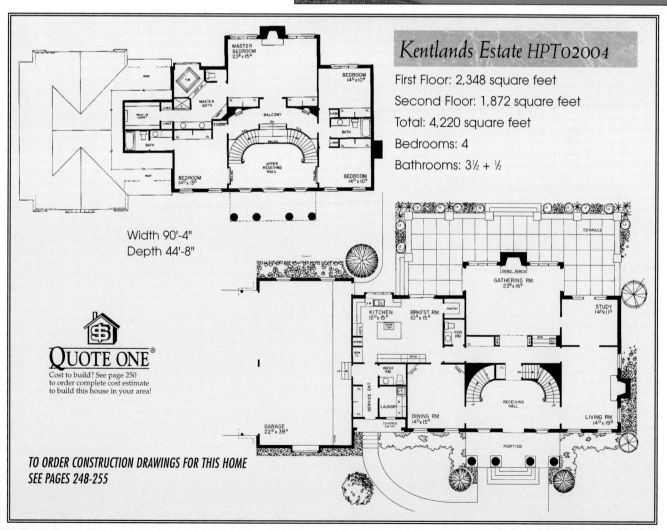

Kentlands Estate HPT02004

First Floor: 2,348 square feet

Second Floor: 1,872 square feet

Total: 4,220 square feet

Bedrooms: 4

Bathrooms: 3½ + ½

Width 90'-4"
Depth 44'-8"

QUOTE ONE®
Cost to build? See page 250
to order complete cost estimate
to build this house in your area!

TO ORDER CONSTRUCTION DRAWINGS FOR THIS HOME SEE PAGES 248-255

A distinctive wrought-iron railing enhances the two-story foyer.

HERMITAGE

DESIGN BY FRANK BETZ ASSOCIATES, INC.

Southern Beauty

The dream-come-true home of designer Frank Betz sinks roots in the heart of the South and takes on the future with an array of sensational amenities.

Frank Betz, President of Frank Betz Associates, Inc., of Atlanta, began planning his own dream house several years ago, combining traditional concepts with an outpouring of his personal inspiration and gifts. The product of this effort is a breathtaking beauty that's much more than just a pretty face. A well-planned interior of open rooms, wide views and smart details provides a comfortable habitat, an inviting place to entertain guests, as well as living space for the family.

A two-story foyer with a barrel-vaulted ceiling creates a sense of spaciousness and makes a fine introduction to a home that's rich with amenities. The central hall features a marble floor with limestone inlay and leads through charming French doors

STREET OF DREAMS
Hermitage

An elegant cut-glass interior window calls up a sense of the past in the owners bath.

Opposite: The rear exterior presents a beautiful double portico, a terrace and a discreetly placed side garage.

Mahogany walls add drama and definition to the two-story library.

to the rear property, which provides a decorative fountain, cascading waterfalls and a grove of trees. Formal rooms include a two-story library with a fireplace and built-in bookshelves, and a spacious dining room with a dome ceiling and lovely triple window. Dinner guests may linger in the library, which provides a coffered ceiling and walls of rich mahogany. A second-floor balcony with a wrought-iron balustrade adds definition and elegant detail.

The dining room leads to a gourmet kitchen through a butler's pantry that includes a wet bar. Nearby, a convenient coat closet is clustered with a laundry and service door to the garage. The kitchen features a walk-in pantry, an angled double sink and access to a private covered porch. An open arrangement of the kitchen, breakfast nook and vaulted family room allows the household cook to participate in conversation while preparing a meal. French doors open the family room to a side covered porch, and a fireplace framed by windows adds warmth.

A first-floor master wing includes the owners suite, a two-story walk-in closet and a vaulted bath with a spa-style tub and an oversized shower. The double-decker wardrobe provides a ship's ladder for easy transit up and down. A radius window brightens the owners bedroom, which is enhanced by a coffered ceiling and decorative columns that lead to a dressing area. A few steps away, the home office or owners study provides a quiet place to read or work.

Upstairs, two family bedrooms share a compartmented bath, while an additional bedroom, or guest suite, has its own bath. Bedroom 3 leads outdoors to a second-floor covered porch, which also opens from Bedroom 4 through French doors. A gallery hall provides a door to the bonus room.

DESIGNER: © Frank Betz Associates, Inc.
BUILDER: Barrington Homes
PHOTOGRAPHS: © Terrebonne Photography

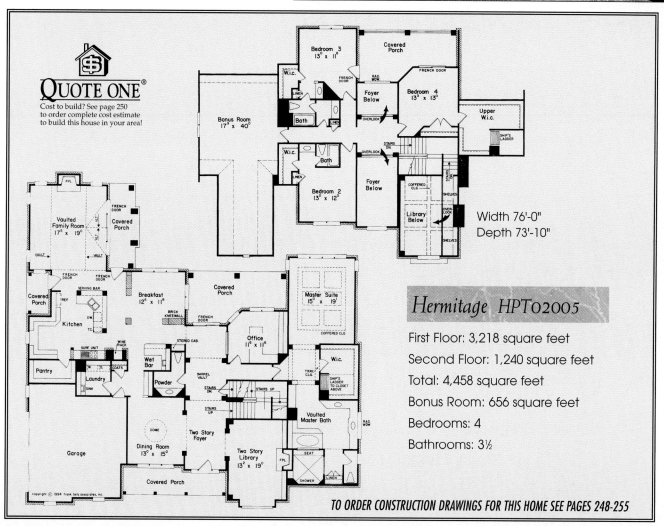

QUOTE ONE®
Cost to build? See page 250 to order complete cost estimate to build this house in your area!

Width 76'-0"
Depth 73'-10"

Hermitage HPT02005

First Floor: 3,218 square feet

Second Floor: 1,240 square feet

Total: 4,458 square feet

Bonus Room: 656 square feet

Bedrooms: 4

Bathrooms: 3½

TO ORDER CONSTRUCTION DRAWINGS FOR THIS HOME SEE PAGES 248-255

STONE POND

DESIGN BY ARCHIVAL DESIGNS, INC.

Simply Perfect

Cathedral ceilings, square columns and a winding stair bring up a rich sense of simpler times and seem perfectly suited for the future.

Stone Pond

Lovely stucco columns and a copper standing-seam roof highlight this stone-and-brick façade. An elegant New World interior starts with a sensational winding staircase, a carved handrail and honey-hued hardwood floor. The gallery hall curves gracefully around the staircase and provides a convenient powder room and coat closet for guests. Additional amenities such as extra built-ins, columns and decorative niches represent the attention to fine detail that's found throughout this striking interior.

An open, two-story formal dining room enjoys front-property views and leads to the gourmet kitchen through the butler's pantry, announced by an archway. Across the foyer, an octagonal formal room easily serves as a library, parlor or den. This room's coffered ceiling and fireplace provide a cozy space to enjoy a good novel or quiet conversation with guests.

Tall windows enhance the multi-level rear exterior and invite natural light into the spacious interior.

Elegant amenities preside in the formal dining room, a place for planned events as well as family meals.

Beyond the foyer, tall windows brighten the two-story family room and bring in a sense of the outdoors, while a fireplace makes the space cozy and warm. The casual living space opens to the kitchen, which has a walk-in pantry and plenty of counter and cabinet space. The center food-prep island counter overlooks a breakfast niche that offers wide views through walls of windows and access to the rear porch. The service entry includes a coat closet that's convenient to the formal dining room and butler's pantry. A side hall leads to a laundry and workstation, then outdoors to a porte cochere.

A few steps away, a private vestibule leads to the owners suite through lovely French doors. The spacious bedroom has a tiered ceiling and a sitting area well lit by windows. Built-in bookshelves and a through-fireplace to the bath provide a cozy setting for reading and a kick-your-shoes-off atmosphere that's as welcome as the flowers in May. A juice bar allows the homeowner to wake up before an early-morning shower or bath, and a dressing room provides a low dresser and leads to a walk-in closet designed for two. The compartmented bath offers a stunning built-in armoire, a makeup vanity and shelves for linen.

The second floor includes two family bedrooms that share a full bath. Each of these bedrooms has a walk-in closet and a private, compartmented lavatory. An additional secondary bedroom offers a spacious private bath with a walk-in closet, whirlpool tub and separate shower. This third bedroom can easily accommodate a guest or live-in relative. A gallery hall leads to a computer room with a dormer and space for a workstation. Nearby, a door provides access to a spacious bonus room with a window.

Windows bring a sense of the outdoors to the two-story family room, while a fireplace gives it a cozy atmosphere.

This home, as shown in the photographs, may differ from the actual blueprints. For more detailed information, please check the floor plans carefully.

A winding staircase highlights the foyer, which provides a powder room and coat closet.

An octagonal ceiling, a fireplace and wide views lend a stately but comfortable feel to the library.

The gourmet kitchen offers a breakfast niche and snack counter for easy family meals.

DESIGNER: © Archival Designs, Inc.
BUILDER: Robert Haymes
INTERIOR DESIGN: Flacks Interiors and
Daniel Reedy Interiors
(page 32, top, only)
PHOTOGRAPHS: © Kerr Studio Inc.

State-of-the-art appliances blend easily with rustic Old World charm in the kitchen.

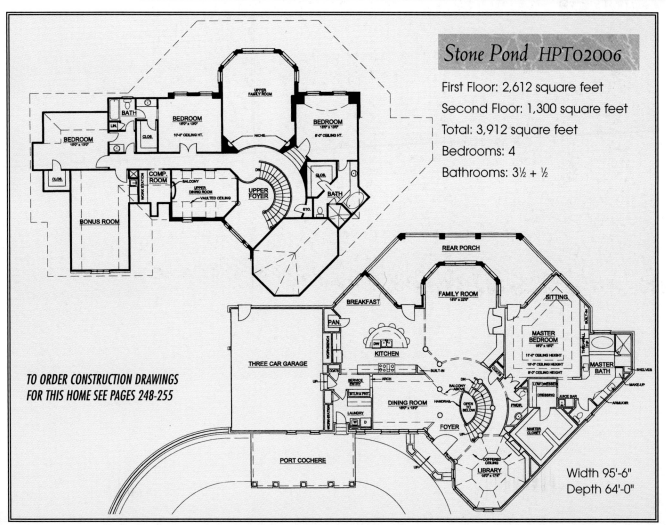

Stone Pond HPT02006

First Floor: 2,612 square feet

Second Floor: 1,300 square feet

Total: 3,912 square feet

Bedrooms: 4

Bathrooms: 3½ + ½

TO ORDER CONSTRUCTION DRAWINGS
FOR THIS HOME SEE PAGES 248-255

Width 95'-6"
Depth 64'-0"

SUMMERPLACE

DESIGN BY PATRICK BARRY, BARRY DESIGN, INC.

This home, as shown in the photographs, may differ from the actual blueprints. For more detailed information, please check the floor plans carefully.

Dash of the Past

A varied palette of historic details brings an uncomplicated elegance and new sizzle to an English Country design.

Wood mold brick with quoins, shuttered double-hung windows, French doors, copper accents and decorative columns along a covered front porch bring modern dash to a home reminiscent of an English country manor. Inside, a fresh color palette of crisp apple greens and yellows contrasts with muted browns and sages. Pineapple House Interior Design, Inc. chose to fill the home with Antique English and French furnishings, which, along with comfortable upholstered pieces, lend a collected, timeless atmosphere to the rooms. A clerestory window and crystal chandelier brighten the two-story foyer, which leads to the formal dining room on the right and the living room or library on the left. A fireplace with a molded wood mantle and bay window are comforting details of this room.

Hardwood floors flow throughout the entire first floor, while unique window treatments complement the floor-to-ceiling windows. Plenty of custom details, such as moldings, tray ceilings, polished brass and built-ins create a sense of heritage in the rooms, enhanced by the special effects of high- and low-voltage lighting. Extra-tall ceilings replace contemporary two-story spaces, returning the house to a traditional interior scale. Past the stairway and gallery hall, the great room features a stacked-stone fireplace and provides space for casual and relaxed entertaining. The adjacent country kitchen provides antiqued cabinets, which match the built-in bookcases in the family room. A

An arch-top window brightens the dining room and offers a pleasing contrast with elegant traditional furniture.

walk-in food pantry and butler's pantry accommodate the cook in the preparation of meals. The bay-window bench in the breakfast nook offers a lovely place to view the rear brick patio. A guest bedroom or study also offers magnificent views of the backyard through a bay window.

Two staircases lead to the upper gallery, with a balcony overlooking the foyer, and to the owners suite and three family bedrooms. In this home, one

A bay window enhances the glow of the fireplace in the living room or library.

A fresh palette creates a pleasing mixture of colors and moods in the great room.

bedroom was converted to a computer room with ample work and closet space. The custom suite includes a spacious private sitting room and built-in entertainment center with four televisions. Decorative columns announce the bedroom, which features a fireplace, built-in bookcases and a floor-to-ceiling bowed window. The interior designers used white-on-white furniture and a fully upholstered

Above: An open arrangement of the great room and breakfast nook invites cozy family gatherings.

Below: The owners suite features a built-in entertainment center and a lavish well-lit bath.

canopied bed to create a soothing, relaxing retreat in these rooms. This retreat provides a deep whirlpool tub—an invitation for the homeowner to relax—that's brightened by a Palladian window. A dual-sink counter offers plenty of storage space, as well as a makeup vanity. A walk-in wardrobe adjoins the master bath and features custom built-ins and natural light from three windows.

The lower level, accessed by stairs near the butler's pantry, provides space for future expansion. A game room, recreation room, kitchenette and additional bedrooms are just some of the possibilities. The three-car garage provides a convenient service entrance that leads to the kitchen, utility room and stairs.

DESIGNER: © Patrick Barry, Barry Design, Inc., Norcross, Georgia
BUILDER: Webco Builders, Inc.
INTERIORS: Pineapple House Interior Design, Inc.
PHOTOGRAPHS: © Visual Solutions Co.

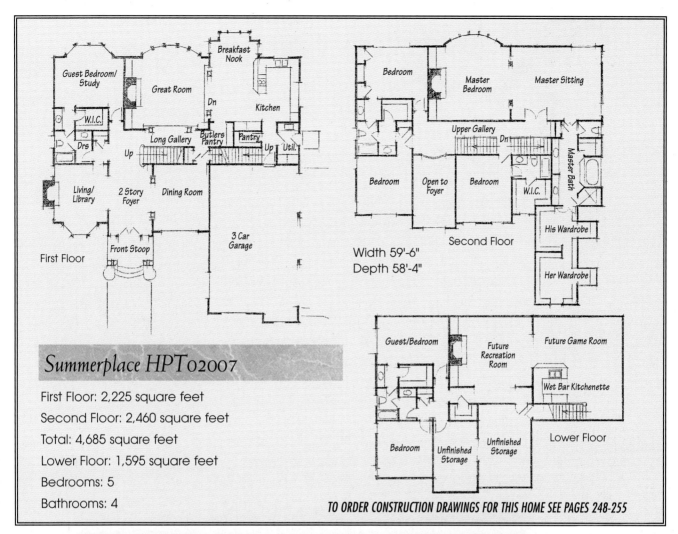

First Floor

Guest Bedroom/Study
Great Room
Breakfast Nook
Dn
Kitchen
W.I.C.
Long Gallery
Butlers Pantry
Pantry
Up
Util.
Drs
Up
Living/Library
2 Story Foyer
Dining Room
3 Car Garage
Front Stoop

Bedroom
Master Bedroom
Master Sitting
Upper Gallery
Dn
Bedroom
Open to Foyer
Bedroom
W.I.C.
Master Bath
His Wardrobe
Her Wardrobe

Second Floor

Width 59'-6"
Depth 58'-4"

Guest/Bedroom
Future Recreation Room
Future Game Room
Wet Bar Kitchenette
Bedroom
Unfinished Storage
Unfinished Storage
Lower Floor

Summerplace HPT02007

First Floor: 2,225 square feet

Second Floor: 2,460 square feet

Total: 4,685 square feet

Lower Floor: 1,595 square feet

Bedrooms: 5

Bathrooms: 4

TO ORDER CONSTRUCTION DRAWINGS FOR THIS HOME SEE PAGES 248-255

Beautiful countertops and cabinetry lend a custom look to the gourmet kitchen.

GRANDHAVEN

DESIGN BY ALAN MASCORD DESIGN ASSOCIATES, INC.

Lap of Luxury

A sensational open interior mixes modern comfort with craftsmanship reminiscent of times gone by.

Varied rooflines, fanciful stucco detailing, multipane Palladian windows and a grand entrance create a façade that exhibits true luxury. The right-angle placement of the three-car garage helps shelter the covered entry, creating a perfect place to welcome visitors. An aura of spaciousness continues inside, where French doors and elegant columns define the foyer. To the left, the formal dining room features a bay window and a stunning coffered ceiling. Tray ceilings, hardwood floors, fluted pillars and high ceilings abound throughout the first floor. The foyer leads directly to the living room, which invites guests to the heart

Arches, gables and varied rooflines lend a gently European flavor to the façade.

This home, as shown in the photographs, may differ from the actual blueprints.
For more detailed information, please check the floor plans carefully.

A stunning transom allows natural light to brighten the elegant foyer.

Opposite: A soaring bay window opens the living room to views of the rear property, inviting a sense of the outdoors.

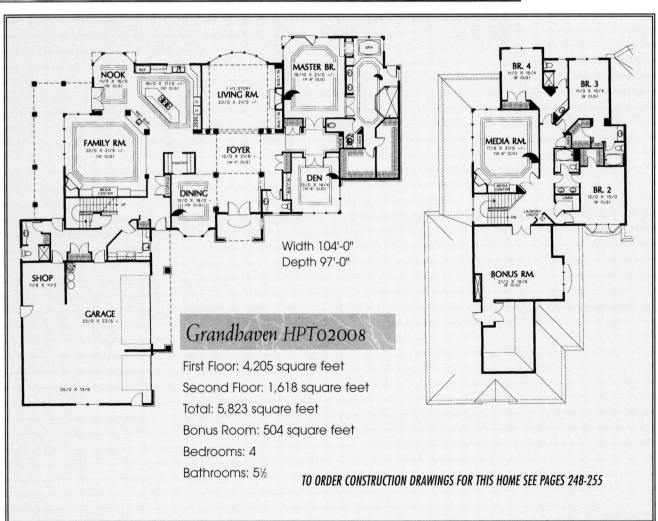

Width 104'-0"
Depth 97'-0"

Grandhaven HPT02008

First Floor: 4,205 square feet

Second Floor: 1,618 square feet

Total: 5,823 square feet

Bonus Room: 504 square feet

Bedrooms: 4

Bathrooms: 5½

TO ORDER CONSTRUCTION DRAWINGS FOR THIS HOME SEE PAGES 248-255

of the home and features a fireplace and a soaring bow window that overlooks the backyard.

Casual living space is just steps away from the living room. A warm and inviting place for family activities, this area's elegant atmosphere and openness to the formal rooms make it ideal for large-scale entertaining. A corner fireplace shares its glow with the kitchen and breakfast nook and complements a distinctive tray ceiling and a wraparound wall of windows. Across the room, a freestanding wet bar helps to define the space for the adjoining kitchen and eating area. The breakfast nook has a bay window and French doors to the outside. The stylish, angled kitchen has a large cooktop island counter and a butler's pantry that leads to the dining room.

French doors announce the first-floor owners suite, which features private access to the rear property and a through-fireplace that's viewed by the spa-style tub. The bath offers a dual-sink vanity, a step-up, oversized shower, a compartmented toilet and bidet, and two walk-in closets. A nearby den provides a quiet place to work or study and features a wraparound wall of windows and built-in bookcases. The second floor includes three family bedrooms, each with its own bath. The media room, a smaller version of the family room below, offers more space in which to entertain. The bonus room provides future space for a game room, home office, additional bedroom or hobby room.

DESIGNER: © Alan Mascord
Design Associates, Inc.
PHOTOGRAPHS: © Bob Greenspan

MULBERRY PLACE

DESIGN BY STEPHEN FULLER,
AMERICAN HOME GALLERY

Twist on Tradition

This stately but comfortable brick home blends Old World charm with a contemporary spirit and floor plan.

Elegance, luxury and state-of-the-art amenities live blissfully together in this 21st-Century home. This creative design features asymmetrical gables and a dramatic brick exterior, enhanced by a recessed entry, twin sets of columns and a graceful arch. Tall arch-top windows decorate the façade and bring natural light into the open interior. Stucco accents and a single dormer add a thoroughly modern spirit to this traditional brick design.

Asymmetrical gables with lovely stucco accents top a series of triple windows.

A sense of elegance prevails in the formal dining room, which provides a wide arch-top window.

Opposite: The breakfast nook provides views and a door to the solarium—a perfect spot to enjoy a cup of tea.

Inside, a dramatic foyer leads to the formal living and dining rooms. A sizable butler's pantry conveniently links the dining room and kitchen, providing perfect facilities for planned events. A sensational formal dining room offers wide views of the front grounds. The gourmet kitchen features a centered food-prep island counter, a corner walk-in pantry and an angled snack counter that overlooks the breakfast nook. This area is designed for casual dining and, with a wall of windows that look out to the solarium, is especially well suited to morning meals. A door to the solarium invites family members to linger, open a book or simply enjoy a cup of tea.

Stunning amenities, such as a tray ceiling, French doors and a fireplace, dress the family room. This spacious room invites cozy gatherings as well as grand-scale entertaining. Doors lead out to the rear porch—a perfect arrangement for after-dinner conversation, stargazing or even dancing. A wet bar, flanked by two sets of privacy doors, allows guests to be served refreshment before being seated.

A private gallery hall with a convenient powder room leads to the owners suite through lovely French doors. The owners bedroom provides a bay window and a door to the rear porch. An angled corner whirlpool tub highlights the homeowners bath. Separate vanities allow privacy even when sharing the bath.

Upstairs, a family bedroom shares a full bath with the spacious sewing room, which easily converts to a playroom. The balcony hall leads to a study nook, a perfect space to surf the Internet or enjoy a quiet read. A home office, or fourth bedroom, features built-ins, a walk-in closet and a triple window.

DESIGNER: © Stephen Fuller,
American Home Gallery
PHOTOGRAPHS: © Dave Dawson Photography

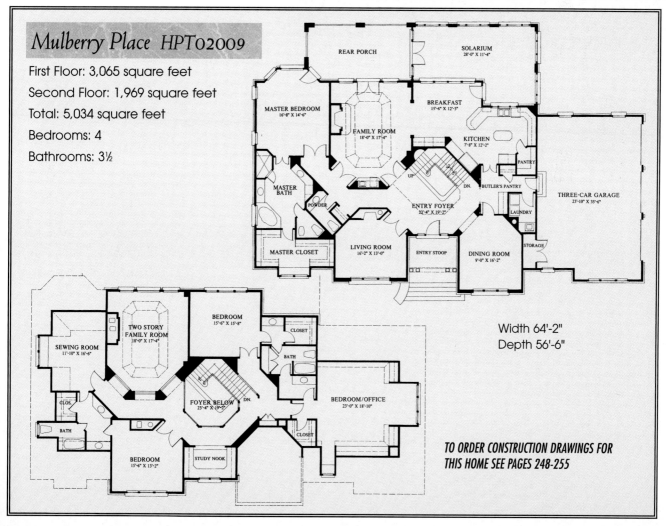

Mulberry Place HPT02009

First Floor: 3,065 square feet

Second Floor: 1,969 square feet

Total: 5,034 square feet

Bedrooms: 4

Bathrooms: 3½

Width 64'-2"
Depth 56'-6"

TO ORDER CONSTRUCTION DRAWINGS FOR THIS HOME SEE PAGES 248-255

La Maison de Rêves

DESIGN BY STEPHEN FULLER, AMERICAN HOME GALLERY

STREET OF DREAMS
La Maison de Rêves

An enchanting staircase
highlights the foyer and
leads up to a spacious
media room.

French Class

*Derived from a classic French vocabulary, this
distinctive design provides a cohesive, refined disposition and charming character in every detail.*

Inspired by the architecture of the French countryside,
La Maison de Rêves incorporates state-of-the-art
technology with a centuries-old style. A stone-and-
brick façade creates an intentionally aged look that is
a perfect complement to the high-tech intercom and
security systems with video monitoring, thermal dou-
ble-glazed windows and energy-efficient heating and
cooling throughout the home. The time-honored tone
of this house is punctuated inside by a satisfying com-
bination of antique and contemporary furniture.

Crosscut travertine floors, arched stacked-stone walls
and a winding wrought-iron staircase give the spacious foyer an Old World flavor. The wide foyer opens
to both the formal dining room and central great
room. The free-flowing design of La Maison de Rêves
allows an impressive style of entertaining, whether formal or casual. In the dining room, fabric-draped walls,
a gold-leafed ceiling and a unique octagonal table

Opposite above: State-of-the-art appliances line the gourmet kitchen, which also provides a food-prep island counter.

Opposite below: French doors brighten the formal dining room and lead outside.

Below: A stone hearth warms the keeping room, enhanced by plenty of natural light.

create a formal yet intimate setting for any occasion. The great room provides a graceful arched entry from the main hallway and access to the rear covered porch. A stone fireplace is the striking centerpiece of this room and is flanked by arched built-ins. A wrought-iron gate guards the entry to the lovely wine niche, where a hand-painted fresco stimulates the imagination.

The exquisite, custom-designed gourmet kitchen includes a stainless-steel range, hood and warming shelves, a silent dishwasher,

This home, as shown in the photographs, may differ from the actual blueprints. For more detailed information, please check the floor plans carefully.

double ovens and a remote ventilator. Distressed brick flooring, a fireplace and an exposed-beam ceiling complete the fabulous charm of this culinary paradise. The breakfast area includes floor-to-ceiling windows that add light and bring a sense of the countryside indoors. Nearby, a keeping room features an impressive stone fireplace that imparts a medieval flavor to the room.

An appreciation of style, space and design is showcased in the dramatic owners suite, complete with a fireplace, sitting area and lavishly draped windows. Tall windows frame the hearth, and a door leads out to a private area of the rear

porch. The luxurious bath provides a sheered-silk ceiling and soft color palette, two walk-in closets, separate vanities and a sunken tub.

On the second floor, a gallery overlooking the foyer leads to the family's sleeping quarters. Each of the secondary bedrooms has separate access to a full bath and plenty of wardrobe space. A bonus

Above: An appreciation of style, space and design is showcased in the dramatic owners suite, complete with a fireplace and sitting area.

Left: A lavish bath with a sheered-silk ceiling and soft color palette provides a soothing retreat for the homeowner.

Opposite: A media room includes built-ins and easily converts to a study or den.

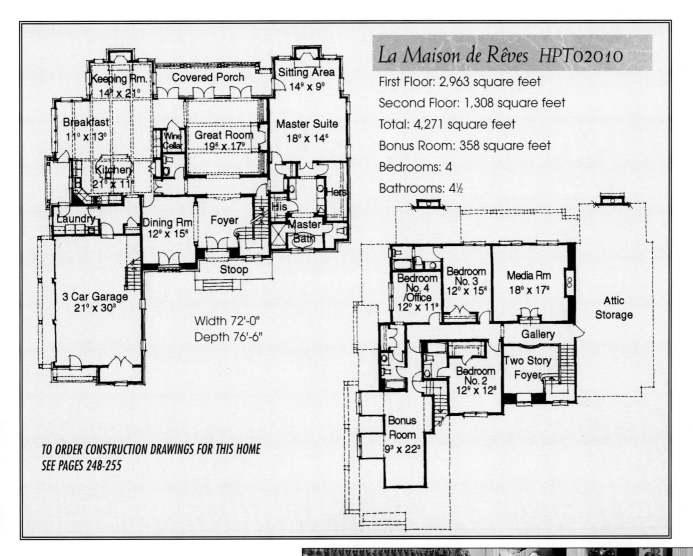

La Maison de Rêves HPT02010

First Floor: 2,963 square feet

Second Floor: 1,308 square feet

Total: 4,271 square feet

Bonus Room: 358 square feet

Bedrooms: 4

Bathrooms: 4½

Floor plan labels (first floor):

Keeping Rm. 14⁰ x 21⁰ · Covered Porch · Sitting Area 14⁹ x 9⁰ · Breakfast 11⁰ x 13⁰ · Wine Cellar · Great Room 19⁶ x 17⁹ · Master Suite 18⁰ x 14⁶ · Kitchen 21⁰ x 11⁶ · Her's · Laundry · Dining Rm 12⁰ x 15⁶ · Foyer · His · Master Bath · 3 Car Garage 21⁰ x 30³ · Stoop

Width 72'-0"
Depth 76'-6"

Floor plan labels (second floor):

Bedroom No. 4 /Office 12⁰ x 11⁹ · Bedroom No. 3 12⁰ x 15⁶ · Media Rm 18⁰ x 17⁹ · Attic Storage · Gallery · Bedroom No. 2 12⁰ x 12⁶ · Two Story Foyer · Bonus Room 9³ x 22³

TO ORDER CONSTRUCTION DRAWINGS FOR THIS HOME
SEE PAGES 248-255

room offers the possibility of a computer nook, home office or play room. At the opposite corner of the second floor, the media room has been customized with a state-of-the-art entertainment center that includes surround sound.

A creative landscape package with centrally controlled irrigation system and site lighting will be the envy of your neighborhood, even if you live in the French countryside. This home is designed with a walkout basement foundation.

DESIGNER: © Stephen Fuller,
American Home Gallery
BUILDER: Mark VII Properties, Inc.
INTERIOR DESIGN: Pineapple House
Interior Design, Inc.
PHOTOGRAPHS: © Visual Solutions Co.
© B. Massey Photographers

COURCHEVEL

DESIGN BY HOME PLANNERS

The New Norman

A spirit of savoir-vivre settles on the soft green hills surrounding a slightly rugged but distinctly comfortable European-style manor.

The castle-like façade of this lovely Norman design speaks well of its French roots but sparkles with a fresh personality as well. Carefully built to look well settled, the country manor nestles in the sylvan hills of a posh, established Midwestern neighborhood. Sunburst fanlights set off historic elements such as Romanesque arches and massive turrets, while organic shades of brick meld with the plush landscape. A fanlight window crowns the massive double doors and invites natural light into the foyer.

This home, as shown in the photographs, may differ from the actual blueprints. For more detailed information, please check the floor plans carefully.

The activities room boasts a balcony that looks out over a wooded canyon.

An enticing simplicity decorates the home, inside and out, and the entire interior flows with an easy panache and timeless spirit. Honey-hued hardwood adds warmth to alabaster-toned walls and ceilings throughout the interior, and carves out soft, pleasing niches in quiet areas such as the study. Arch-top windows and skylights splash the indoors with wide views of nature and dreamy light, which, when mixed with the French-inspired architecture, create a sense of romance and individuality.

A distinctive covered entry leads to a well-lit, two-story foyer, with a graceful, gently curved staircase and a thoughtfully placed powder room. The plan opens to a formal dining room and to a step-down gathering room, which features a raised-hearth fireplace and panoramic views of the back property. A generous study occupies the base of the right turret and provides excellent outdoor views.

Nearby, a well-organized kitchen includes an island workstation, a planning desk and a sizable morning room with a private porch.

Above: Open planning allows the foyer to share outdoor views through the gathering room, which has access to the entertainment terrace.

Left: A gently curved hardwood balustrade lines the staircase, which leads to the spacious sleeping quarters.

Opposite: The owners bedroom has its own hearth and enjoys triple-window views.

The open kitchen dominates the left wing of this dream home and separates the octagonal dining room from the morning room. Windows and skylights brighten the eating area while glass doors lead out to the terrace. A clutter room, wash room and laundry complete this wing.

A vestibule with a niche for curios introduces a generous owners wing. The bedroom has a sitting area with a fireplace and a lovely triple window, which looks out to the rear terrace. The suite features a deluxe spa and exercise room, harbored in a bumped-out nook with access to a private covered porch. Two walk-in closets, a dressing room with a double-bowl vanity, and a whirlpool tub highlight the bath.

The second floor includes four secondary bedrooms, four baths and an activities room that has a piano niche, morning kitchen and fireplace. An entertainment center or home theater could make this the most popular room in the house. A triangular balcony overlooks the terrace.

DESIGNER: © Home Planners
PHOTOGRAPHS: © Andrew D. Lautman

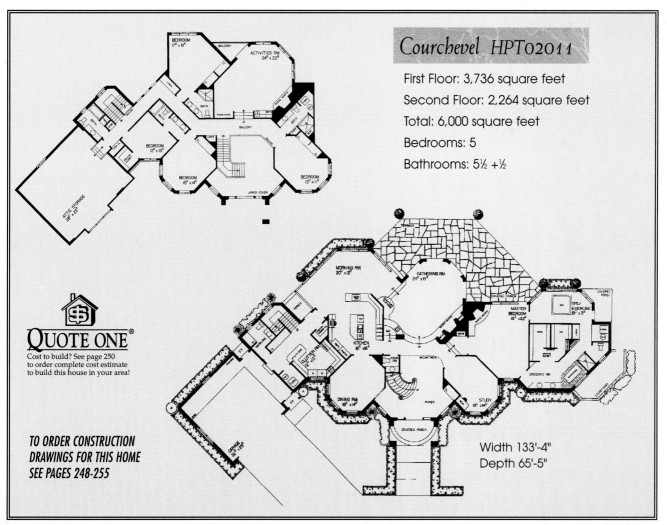

Courchevel HPT02011

First Floor: 3,736 square feet

Second Floor: 2,264 square feet

Total: 6,000 square feet

Bedrooms: 5

Bathrooms: 5½ +½

QUOTE ONE®

Cost to build? See page 250 to order complete cost estimate to build this house in your area!

TO ORDER CONSTRUCTION DRAWINGS FOR THIS HOME SEE PAGES 248-255

Width 133'-4"
Depth 65'-5"

VERSAILLES

DESIGN BY LIVING CONCEPTS HOME PLANNING

Present Perfect

Rich textures and plucky hues weave a tantalizing mix of rustic and modern rooms, made for the luxury of comfort.

This French country estate displays a beautiful stone façade, gabled roof, multi-paned, arched casement windows with shutters, and stately stone chimneys. An arched loggia and double French doors with a transom window lead to the two-story foyer, which is brightened by the dormer window above. Visitors are greeted with the warm light of a crystal and wrought-iron chandelier and a stunning interior vista of a curving stairway with a hardwood balustrade. Hardwood floors, archways, raised ceilings and recessed lighting are found throughout the first floor.

Dine in luxury, warmed by the glow of a cast-stone fireplace, flanked by built-in hutches with detailed molding. The study provides built-in bookcases, its own fire-

STREET OF DREAMS
Versailles

place and access to the owners suite. A nearby powder room accommodates guests and maintains privacy for the owners suite. In the grand room, a two-story beam ceiling enhances a wall of windows, which brings in plenty of natural light. Built-in bookcases flank a marble fireplace, and French doors lead to the rear terrace—a perfect arrangement for planned entertaining or cozy gatherings. A side staircase provides convenient access to the second-floor home theater.

A well-organized kitchen features a food-prep island counter, walk-in pantry and plenty of cabinet space. Recessed lighting, dual sinks and tile counters provide an ideal cooking area. A morning bay adjoins the kitchen and gathering room and offers views of the terrace. Detailed molding, built-in cabinetry, a fireplace and access to the terrace make the gathering room an inviting place for the family.

A lovely triple window highlights the owners suite, which provides a morning kitchen and private access to the study. Separate walk-in closets and dressing areas allow privacy to the owners. The spacious bath features a knee-space

A faux-finished cast-stone fireplace surround and a sheet-rock chimney breast give this two-story grand room a truly grand appearance.

Opposite: Finely detailed cabinets flank the cast-stone fireplace surround that boasts a marble finish.

Draped safari cloth, a reproduction French-style daybed and a waterstain scumble effect on the walls enhance the Old World bedroom.

vanity, angled shower and a bumped-out tub with a bay window. Upstairs, each of the three bedroom suites has a walk-in closet and a private bath. Above the three-car garage, a full kitchen and bath make up a private apartment, perfect for a maid's quarters, or live-in relatives.

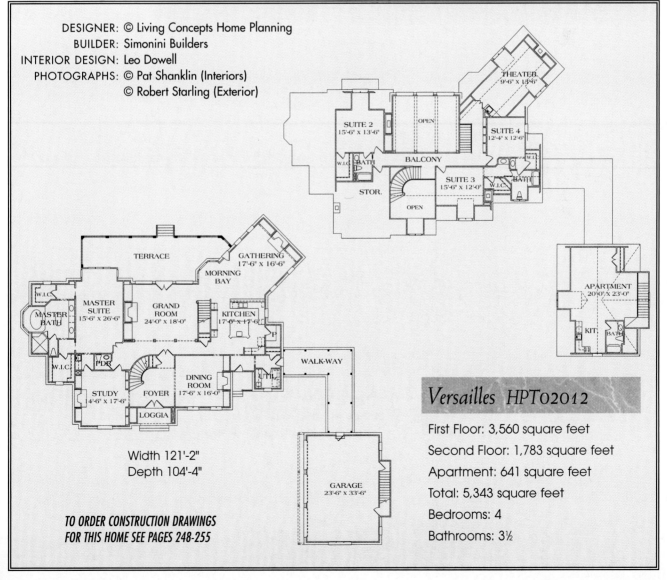

DESIGNER: © Living Concepts Home Planning
BUILDER: Simonini Builders
INTERIOR DESIGN: Leo Dowell
PHOTOGRAPHS: © Pat Shanklin (Interiors)
© Robert Starling (Exterior)

THEATER
9'-6" x 15'-6"

SUITE 2
15'-6" x 13'-6"

OPEN

SUITE 4
12'-4" x 12'-6"

W.I.C. BATH

BALCONY

W.I.C.

STOR.

SUITE 3
15'-6" x 12'-0"

BATH

W.I.C.

OPEN

APARTMENT
20'-0" x 23'-0"

KIT.

BATH

TERRACE

GATHERING
17'-6" x 16'-6"

MORNING BAY

W.I.C.

MASTER SUITE
15'-6" x 26'-6"

GRAND ROOM
24'-0" x 18'-0"

KITCHEN
17'-6" x 17'-6"

MASTER BATH

W.I.C.

PDR

STUDY
14'-6" x 17'-6"

FOYER

DINING ROOM
17'-6" x 16'-0"

UTIL.

WALK-WAY

LOGGIA

GARAGE
23'-6" x 33'-6"

Width 121'-2"
Depth 104'-4"

Versailles HPT02012

First Floor: 3,560 square feet
Second Floor: 1,783 square feet
Apartment: 641 square feet
Total: 5,343 square feet
Bedrooms: 4
Bathrooms: 3½

TO ORDER CONSTRUCTION DRAWINGS
FOR THIS HOME SEE PAGES 248-255

BRAVEHEART

DESIGN BY SCHAUMBERG ARCHITECTS, INC.

Revival Instincts

With picturesque gables and turrets, this castle-like European design boasts up-to-date amenities and simmers with a tasteful blend of past and present.

This modern masterpiece mixes artistic stone masonry with brick to create a unique façade influenced by elements of Gothic, Romanesque and Tudor architecture. A two-story turret protects one corner of this home and summons images of fairy-tale palaces. The asymmetrical roof embodies many different styles and complements hand-trawled walls and beveled-glass French exterior doors.

This home, as shown in the photographs, may differ from the actual blueprints. For more detailed information, please check the floor plans carefully.

A Gothic-style window and a stately mantel define the living room.

This sensational manor comprises over 7,600 square feet of exquisite craftsmanship and unmatched elegance. A gently curving staircase graced with a hand-forged wrought-iron railing highlights the two-story foyer, which also features antique hardwood flooring. The formal dining room opens directly from the foyer and is illuminated by a magnificent chandelier and natural light from a tall Gothic window. The opposite side of the foyer leads to the library and conservatory, where the beautiful ceilings are decorated with authentic trim pieces. The conservatory occupies the lower part the turret and provides wide views of the outdoors.

Decorative columns help define the formal living room, which provides a Gothic cathedral window and stately custom fireplace. A hospitable formality reigns in the nearby piano room, where the musician of the family can spend countless hours playing Mozart or Chopin. Double French doors allow access to the rear porch and admit sunlight to inspire the artistic creativity of any family member.

A spectacular owners suite includes a fireplace framed by tall windows, imported pattern wool carpeting and a simply remarkable bath. An oversized circular

The piano room offers a timeless décor and an atmosphere of relaxed elegance—a true comfort zone.

The one-of-a-kind family room offers extensive vaulted ceilings and a stone fireplace.

shower features a garden wall, and the nearby island whirlpool tub allows a relaxing soak for the busy homeowner. Separate vanities, two walk-in closets and a compartmented toilet complete this retreat.

The right half of the home is devoted to informal living spaces. A spacious kitchen features a grand island counter, separate snack bar and an ample walk-in pantry. The breakfast room is the perfect place for taking morning coffee and catching up on the news. The largest room in the plan is the family room. Here, a vaulted wood ceiling with distressed wood beams complements a custom stone fireplace and twin sets of French doors leading outside.

Near the family room, a cozy guest suite enjoys a secluded corner of the plan and provides

Above: The homeowners retreat includes an inviting bath with lavish but comfortable amenities.

Opposite: Hardwood floors and Gothic windows enhance the formal rooms of this lovely castle.

A masterpiece mantel highlights the owners bedroom—a relaxing haven far from the bumps and beeps of city life.

a walk-in closet, a cabana bath and wide views. This wing includes a large utility room for storage and laundry.

The central staircase leads from the foyer to the waiting area for an impressive home theater. This customized chamber includes a ten-foot screen, THX, an AC3 digital sound system and the latest technology of DVDs and laser disks. The theater hall leads to the entrance of a spacious game room, which has a billiard and card table.

DESIGNER: © Schaumberg Architects, Inc.,
Fort Worth, Texas
BUILDER: Majesty Homes
INTERIOR DESIGN: The Design Studio of Gabberts
PHOTOGRAPHS: © Visual Solutions Co.

Braveheart HPT02013

First Floor: 4,996 square feet

Second Floor: 2,610 square feet

Total: 7,606 square feet

Bedrooms: 5

Bathrooms: 5½ + ½

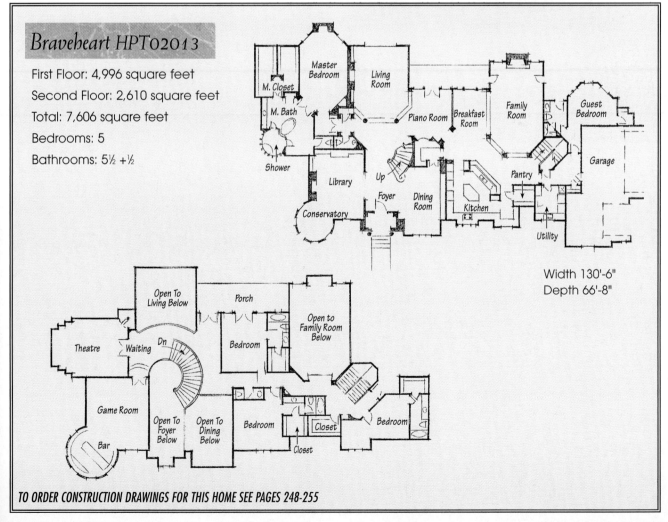

Width 130'-6"
Depth 66'-8"

TO ORDER CONSTRUCTION DRAWINGS FOR THIS HOME SEE PAGES 248-255

THE MANSION

DESIGN BY RUSBOURNE DESIGN LTD.

Simple Geometry

Both contemporary and provincial, the unique lines of this comfortable French Country estate come together in a satisfying mix of form and function.

This stunning manor calls up a sense of the past yet invites a 21st-Century lifestyle, with vaulted interior vistas, floor-to-ceiling windows and plenty of space for both

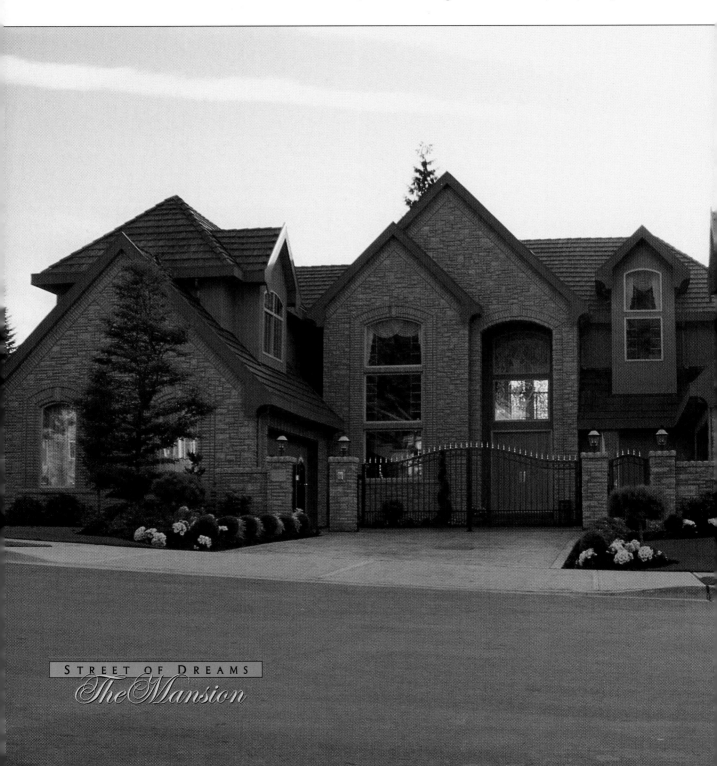

STREET OF DREAMS
The Mansion

Rich hues lend a sense of comfort and elegance to the living room.

traditional and casual entertaining. The courtyard is flanked by two garages and leads to a grand recessed entry that offers a royal welcome to guests. A two-story foyer features an upper-level gallery overlook and a grand winding staircase that leads to an elegant sleeping zone.

The formal wing includes a quiet den with a bay window and an open arrangement of the living and dining rooms. A sculptured mantle with ornate detailing sets off the living room, which is ingeniously defined and separated from the dining room by a piano portico. Opulent textures, geometric ceiling relief and faux finishes add quality and detail throughout the home. A splendid chandelier, suspended from a coffered ceiling, enhances the living room's luxurious environment, rendered in tones of eggplant and cream.

A second-floor gallery and balustrade overlooks the foyer's stunning granite floor.

A well-equipped servery leads to the gourmet kitchen, a classic blend of function and aesthetics, providing fine bird's-eye maple cabinets that trace a gently curved line to a hidden walk-in pantry. Green granite countertops provide efficient work-spaces of substance. The morning nook offers a wide view of the deck and rear property through a curved wall of glass. Arches and columns open the nook to

Delicate details add a measure of elegance to the gallery's wrought-iron balustrade.

A wide, divided-light window provides drama and detail to the den.

This home, as shown in the photographs, may differ from the actual blueprints. For more detailed information, please che the floor plans carefully.

Above: Double doors open to the home theater from the lounge, bar and dance floor.

Inset: A gallery hall provides a grand introduction to the formal living room.

Opposite: A sizable servery facilitates crowd-size events as well as casual gatherings.

the family room, which has a fireplace and its own view of the deck. A convenient side staircase provides family members with access to the kitchen and casual living space.

Upstairs, a rambling owners suite provides a private balcony and morning kitchen. The bath features a bumped-out whirlpool tub as well as a spectacular circular shower with overlapping curved glass panels and chiseled sculpted edges. A pocket privacy door conceals a compartmented toilet and bidet. The owners bedroom offers sitting and sleeping space and an overlook to the living room, which allows a view of the fireplace. Secondary sleeping quarters include two family bedrooms that share a bath. Each of these bedrooms has a special window treatment: a bay window in one bedroom and a box-bay window in the other. A spacious guest suite also resides on this floor.

The comfort and quality of this home extend far beyond the visual. A customized version of the basement boasts a home theater with French doors that lead to a private lounge with a bar, cork dance floor, karaoke system and a THX 100-inch big-screen TV. The billiards room provides wide views and a door to the covered patio.

DESIGNER: © Rusbourne Design Ltd.
Port Moody, British Columbia
BUILDER: Emerald Homes
INTERIOR DESIGN: Fine Lines Interiors
FURNISHINGS: Paramount Furniture
PHOTOGRAPHS: © Bizzo Photography

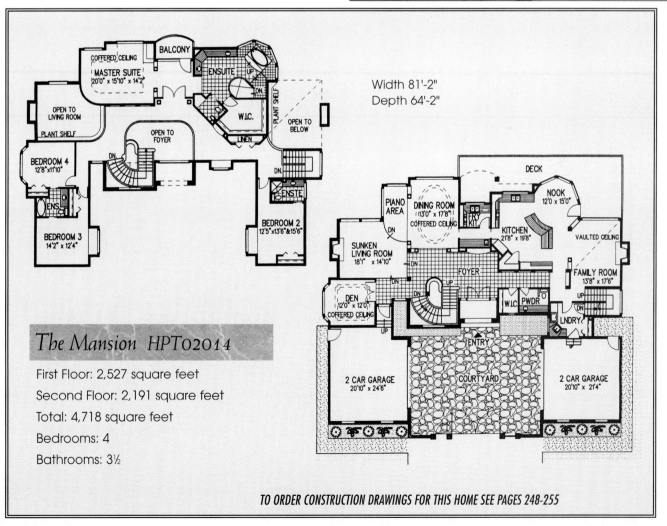

Width 81'-2"
Depth 64'-2"

The Mansion HPT02014

First Floor: 2,527 square feet

Second Floor: 2,191 square feet

Total: 4,718 square feet

Bedrooms: 4

Bathrooms: 3½

TO ORDER CONSTRUCTION DRAWINGS FOR THIS HOME SEE PAGES 248-255

CHAMBORD

DESIGN BY SULLIVAN/STEVENS & HENRY ASSOCIATES, INC.

STREET OF DREAMS
Chambord

Hip Chateau

Time-honored details step into the future with a way-past-cool façade and a bang-up-to-date interior that offers all the comforts of home.

From the outside, Chambord appears both familiar and fresh, as if its stately countenance had sprouted up between comely chateaux along the Loire, both fitting and revising the fairyland look of the region. Decorative quoins, varied window treatments and a covered entryway create curb appeal and present a warm welcome to this lovely home. Mahogany double doors open to a magnificent foyer, which features massive stone columns and a floating staircase of ornamental iron. Recessed, high-intensity projector lighting showcases artwork and adds a sense of drama to handcrafted molding and heated European limestone floors. State-of-the-art electronics installed in this version of the plan include video security, telephone and computer systems that will easily handle multimedia requirements well into the 21st Century.

Throughout the interior, a thoughtful mix of antiques and modern furnishings create a tasteful blend of 18th-Century charm and up-to-the-minute amenities. Distinctive faux finishes add drama to cabinets and custom moldings, while crafted details enhance every area of the home. A massive hand-carved mantel over the fireplace in the living room lends a European flavor to the formal area. Tall windows framed by plush drapes offer views to the front property and the stunning courtyard. Across the foyer, a beautiful arched entry

This home, as shown in the photographs, may differ from the actual blueprints. For more detailed information, please check the floor plans carefully.

of walnut and hand-made leaded glass opens to the library, which is finished in raised-block paneling of American black walnut. This room may also be used as a parlor or den and easily converts to a guest room.

The foyer leads past the staircase to gallery halls that lead to the owners retreat and beyond the dining room to the family living space. To the rear of the plan, an open arrangement of the kitchen, breakfast bay and family room create a cozy, comfortable area that invites both solitude and shared activities. Picturesque windows in the breakfast and family rooms offer sweeping views to the private courtyard, including a pool, spa and outdoor kitchen. The family room boasts a stone fireplace, built-ins and a tray ceiling, and opens to a covered terrace, which has a unique summer kitchen, including a gas grill with infrared rotisserie, dual-burner range and sink.

A solid granite slab tops the counters in the gourmet kitchen, bar, powder room and niches. Hand-rubbed antiqued cabinets with elegant moldings live happily with thoroughly modern appliances. A stove-top island counter, two pantries and access to the three-car garage are features every cook will appreciate. A wine rack alcove leads

Left: An elegant two-story foyer features mahogany doors and a floating staircase with an ornamental iron balustrade.

Above: Raised-block paneling of American black walnut finishes the library—a room that easily converts to a parlor or study.

Right: The living room provides a fireplace and access to the back property through lovely French doors.

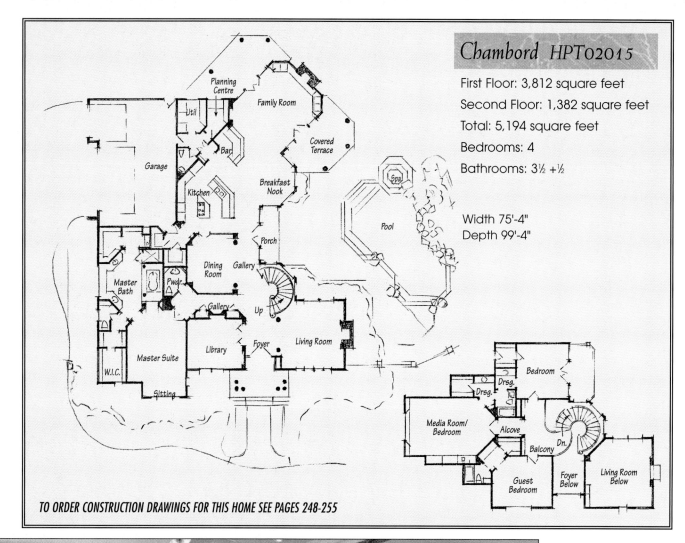

Chambord HPT02015

First Floor: 3,812 square feet

Second Floor: 1,382 square feet

Total: 5,194 square feet

Bedrooms: 4

Bathrooms: 3½ + ½

Width 75'-4"
Depth 99'-4"

Planning Centre

Family Room

Util

Bar

Covered Terrace

Garage

Kitchen

Breakfast Nook

Spa

Porch

Pool

Dining Room

Gallery

Master Bath

Pwdr.

Up

Gallery

Library

Foyer

Living Room

Master Suite

W.I.C.

Sitting

Bedroom

Drsg.

Drsg.

Media Room/ Bedroom

Alcove

Dn.

Balcony

Guest Bedroom

Foyer Below

Living Room Below

TO ORDER CONSTRUCTION DRAWINGS FOR THIS HOME SEE PAGES 248-255

Left: The owners bedroom features a sitting area with a stunning view of the front property.

Opposite above: Casual living space includes a family room that's warmed by a fireplace and plenty of views.

Opposite below: Stone columns frame an elegant step-up tub in the owners bath.

to a powder room, the utility room and planning center.

The owners suite provides a sitting area and generous open space in the bedroom. The bath features heated floors, marble walls, elegant arched openings and a steam shower with an etched butt-glass enclosure. Separate walk-in closets and a dual-sink vanity with makeup table complete this comforting retreat. Upstairs, a balcony hall overlooks the foyer and connects the secondary bedrooms. One of the bedrooms opens to an outdoor terrace and shares its bath with the media room, which features a recessed projector screen, cove lighting, media cabinets, bar, refrigerator and microwave.

DESIGNER: © Sullivan/Stevens & Henry
Associates, Inc., Houston, Texas
BUILDER: Charles Perryman Fine Homes
INTERIOR DESIGN: The Market
PHOTOGRAPHS: © Visual Solutions Co.

BRINDIAMO ALLA VITA

DESIGN BY RICHARD DRUMMOND DAVIS

European Country Cool

An elegant design with a dramatic Italian influence blends the ease of luxury with the comfortable feeling of home.

STREET OF DREAMS
Brindiamo Alla Vita

A massive wood and iron gate adorns the magnificent entry courtyard.

A stunning mix of brick, stucco and distinctive rock create this well-proportioned exterior, which is set off by a magnificent entry courtyard and a massive wood and iron gate. The multi-pitch roof lends itself to a villa-style appearance, while a beautifully formalized scalloped shell and a voluted console form an authentic stone fountain, which adds to the Italian charm. A covered porch with fine lighting shields the wood and glass double-door entry. Raised-panel doors and 1920-era renaissance trim create an estate atmosphere, while thoughtfully placed accent lighting creates drama with highly controlled beams of light. A future-proof interactive network panel distributes high-performance electronic signals, providing security and comfort throughout the home.

A nicely appointed kitchen provides a cooktop island counter, stunning cabinetry and hardwood floors.

Tall windows in the formal dining room allow views of the side and rear properties.

Windows on two floors illuminate the foyer, which features a grand U-shaped staircase leading to secondary sleeping quarters. A wide hallway increases the space of the already open design, and a small niche holds two closets for coat storage and a handy powder room. Double doors lead into the classic library adorned with beautiful wood shelving and hardwood floors. A hidden bar is thoughtfully placed between the library and living room for shared access. The living room features a centerpiece wood-burning fireplace and three tall windows that provide pleasant views of the outdoors.

A gallery hall leads beyond the foyer to the stately formal dining room. Hardwood floors and an elegant chandelier make this room ideal for traditional events. A butler's pantry and walk-in coat closet lead to a nicely appointed kitchen. The culinary artist of the family will appreciate the cooktop island counter and ample cabinet space. The breakfast room boasts a beautiful wood floor, charming chandelier and rich cabinetry.

Twenty-foot-high, vaulted beamed ceilings crown the family room—a comfortable place for gatherings grand or cozy. A centered fireplace flanked by built-ins provides definition and warmth to this inviting room. Two sets of double doors lead to separate covered porches and a garden area. A rear staircase allows easy access to the secondary sleeping quarters as well as the media room or home theater.

The luxurious first-floor master suite offers a spacious sleeping chamber, announced by a double-door entrance. The owners suite also features a fireplace, lovely wood floors and a wall of glass that allows views to the rear property. Pewter trim and bath

The classic library is rich in beautiful wood shelving and provides a hidden bar.

accessories enhance the lavish bath, which includes two walk-in closets, two vanities, a whirlpool bath and a separate shower. Upstairs, three spacious suites pamper each family member with a walk-in closet and private bath. The upper gallery hall provides stunning views of the courtyard and leads down to the entry.

The media room offers a barrel-vaulted ceiling, which commands attention in this high-tech zone. This large area includes an inviting home theater, plenty of built-ins and a rear staircase that leads up to a bonus room over the three-car garage. This space is available for future development and perfectly suited for use as a recreation room, mother-in-law suite, a storeroom for the family heirlooms or an exercise room.

DESIGNER: © Richard Drummond Davis, Dallas, Texas
BUILDER: David Lewis Builders, Inc.
INTERIOR DESIGN: G. Bradley Alford & Associates, Inc.
PHOTOGRAPHS: © Visual Solutions Co.

A breakfast room shares views of the courtyard with the kitchen.

Opposite: Double doors lead to the owners suite, which combines a cozy gas fireplace and a sense of the outdoors brought in by a box-bay window.

Rows of windows help to define the court-yard and allow plenty of natural light within.

This home, as shown in the photographs, may differ from the actual blueprint. For more detailed information, please check the floor plans carefully.

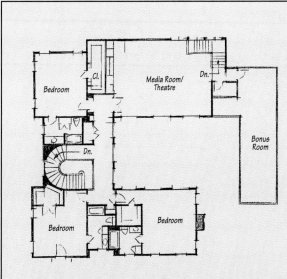

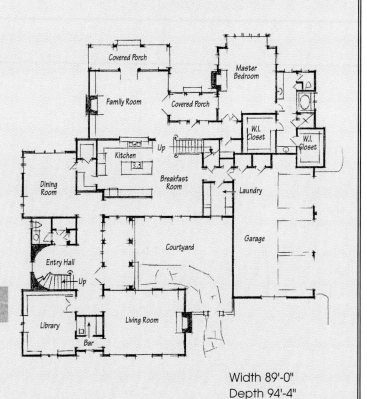

Brindiamo Alla Vita HPT02016

First Floor: 4,188 square feet

Second Floor: 2,350 square feet

Total: 6,538 square feet

Bedrooms: 4

Bathrooms: 4½ + ½

Width 89'-0"

Depth 94'-4"

TO ORDER CONSTRUCTION DRAWINGS FOR THIS HOME SEE PAGES 248-255

THE EMPRESS

DESIGN BY SELECT HOME DESIGNS

Classic Revival

Mastercrafted in grand European tradition, this design successfully combines a gracious past with the innovative comforts of the future.

STREET OF DREAMS
The Empress

This grand, two-story European design is adorned with a façade of stucco and brick, and appointed with details for gracious living. Gently cascading rooflines merge with the massed stone portico. Understated neoclassical lines conceal the harmonious and sophisticated open space within. Designer Steve Riley's goal was to mix the traditional exterior with neoclassical elements of the interior. Architectural details such as stately obelisk pedestals make this interpretation of the designer's vision unique. The luxurious interior is introduced by aged bronze slate, a reflection of the careful attention to detail provided by the interior design firm, Different Designs.

The rooms project a blissful mix of tradition and comfort. A lovely tray ceiling and a fireplace both warm and define the living room. The formal dining room features a bay window that brightens both of the formal rooms during daylight hours. An ample butler's pantry connects the dining room with a well-appointed gourmet kitchen, which adjoins a separate work area. The kitchen reflects the classical design elements of the formal rooms' furnishings. Custom-stained maple cabinets with black granite countertops will satisfy the culinary artist's needs. A large island counter provides a cooktop as well as plenty of space for food preparation. The tile floor extends to the breakfast nook, which has access to the rear property through French doors. Decorative columns open this area to the family room, where a fireplace, aquarium and entertainment center make this an inviting gathering place.

The upper gallery provides a descending view of the family room's magnificent nine-teen-foot slate fireplace. The floor-to-ceiling arch-top window frames the cascading waterfall located in the garden beyond. A gallery hall leads to the owners suite, a retreat that's bathed in natural light. The sense of spaciousness is enhanced by a triple window and vaulted ceiling, and made cozy by a peninsula fireplace. The sitting area adjoins a luxurious ensuite that features an aero-pulse massage tub and a steam-room shower with a seat.

The family room provides a fireplace, media center and aquarium.

This home, as shown in the photographs, may differ from the actual blueprints. For more detailed information, please check the floor plans carefully.

The kitchen reflects design
elements of the living- and
dining-room furnishings.

A guest suite with a win-
dow seat, walk-in closet
and private bath opens
to a gallery hall with a
balcony overlook to the
foyer and family room.
Children's theme rooms
become the dream of
any pre-teen son or
daughter. The interior
design firm, Different
Designs, provided one
of the bedrooms with a
sophisticated country
feeling and carried over

An elegant bay window with
a seat enhances the den,
which also provides space
for a computer center.

The owners ensuite is a pampering retreat, complete with a makeup vanity, soaking tub, steam shower and skylight.

the western theme of the other secondary bedroom into the guest suite.

On the lower floor, a dramatic but comfortable informal entertainment area is an inviting place to enjoy a game of billiards before lounging in the home theater, which is equipped with high-tech audio-visual equipment and a large karaoke screen. The rustic wine cellar features hand-painted wall and floor finish-

A three-sided fireplace warms the owners bedroom and a sitting area, which has a vaulted ceiling.

es. Nearby, an exercise room provides an area for lifting weights or running the treadmill. The hobby room has space for built-ins, and the media room offers a wet bar and a built-in entertainment center.

DESIGNER: © Select Home Designs
BUILDER: Michael Tung, T.S.M. Homes
INTERIOR DESIGN: Different Designs
FURNISHINGS: Brougham Interiors
PHOTOGRAPHS: © Bizzo Photography

The lower-floor media room features a built-in media center.

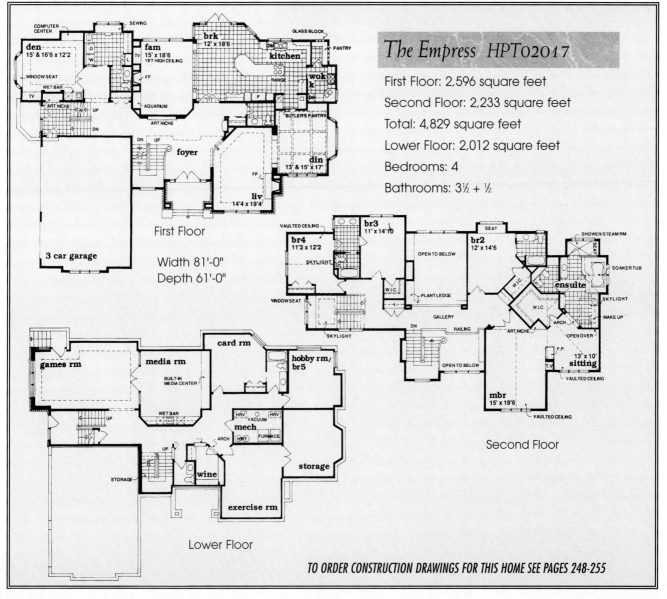

The Empress HPT02017

First Floor: 2,596 square feet

Second Floor: 2,233 square feet

Total: 4,829 square feet

Lower Floor: 2,012 square feet

Bedrooms: 4

Bathrooms: 3½ + ½

First Floor

Width 81'-0"
Depth 61'-0"

Second Floor

Lower Floor

TO ORDER CONSTRUCTION DRAWINGS FOR THIS HOME SEE PAGES 248-255

L'Auberge

DESIGN BY LARRY E. BELK DESIGNS

High Style

Doric columns and elegant arches topped by capstones make a bold statement for the entry of this spectacular European-style home.

Dramatic entry arches create an aura of elegance in the front of the home.

This home, as shown in the photographs, may differ from the actual blueprints. For more detailed information, please check the floor plans carefully.

An entry framed by Doric columns complements a stunning brick-and-stucco façade, creating a warm welcome to this contemporary European-style home. Various window shapes and decorative lintels provide definition and add interest to the exterior. A leaded-glass entry framed with sidelights leads to the two-story foyer, which is also brightened by two Palladian windows and an intricate chandelier. A grand staircase of wood and wrought iron graces the two-story foyer and a balcony rail provides an overlook. Detailed molding, ten-foot ceilings and transoms are found throughout the first floor. Hard wood floors flow through the foyer, dining room, living room and owners bedroom, while tiles spread through the family room, kitchen and breakfast nook.

The living room offers a two-story ceiling and two sets of French

STREET OF DREAMS
L'Auberge

The first-floor owners suite has a tray ceiling, lavish bath and two walk-in closets.

The living room is bathed in natural light from the foyer and two sets of French doors.

A grand staircase highlights the foyer, well lit by Palladian-style windows and a leaded-glass entry framed by sidelights.

doors, which create a sense of spaciousness and help bring in the outdoors. Hardwood floors add elegance to this formal space and provide flow from the foyer. Decorative columns define the entrance to the room from the central gallery hall, which leads to the owners wing on the left and to the casual living area, service entrance and utility room on the right.

Just off the foyer, graceful arches and a decorative column open to the formal dining room, which also features two large windows facing the front yard. The kitchen offers a pantry and snack bar that seats four. Exquisite hardwood cabinetry, marble countertops and a ceramic-tile floor create a regal sense of elegance in the gourmet kitchen. The breakfast nook overlooks the rear yard through a beautiful bay window, which provides natural light to the kitchen as well. A fireplace warms the family room and enhances the light brought in by three windows and a French door that leads to the rear porch. A nearby powder room is convenient for guests. The adjoining room provides a laundry and a service entrance from the garage.

At the opposite side of the plan, a spacious owners suite offers generous amenities, including great views of the rear property. A sumptuous bath features a knee-space vanity, separate lavatories, two walk-in closets and an angled whirlpool tub with a window. The oversized shower includes a seat. The bedroom has a tray ceiling and is

Above: Graceful arches announce the elegant formal dining room, which provides arched windows that allow views to the rear property.

Left: Exquisite cabinetry and ceramic floors lend a classic sense of style to the gourmet kitchen.

rich with classic details such as moldings and cornices.

Upstairs, a balcony hall overlooks both the foyer and living room and connects secondary sleeping quarters with two full baths and a game room. One of the family bedrooms has a walk-in closet and a bay window that offers views to the rear property. The game room provides space for hobbies, a media center, office or study and includes an expandable area for future development.

DESIGNER: © Larry E. Belk Designs
PHOTOGRAPHS: © Scott Ramsey,
        Courtesy Larry E. Belk Designs

The owners bath has a knee-space vanity and separate lavatories.

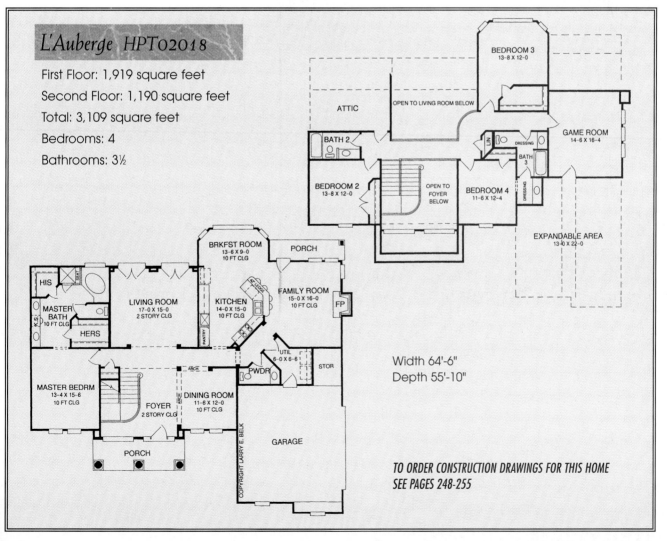

L'Auberge HPT02018

First Floor: 1,919 square feet

Second Floor: 1,190 square feet

Total: 3,109 square feet

Bedrooms: 4

Bathrooms: 3½

Width 64'-6"
Depth 55'-10"

TO ORDER CONSTRUCTION DRAWINGS FOR THIS HOME SEE PAGES 248-255

WATERSONG

DESIGN BY GREG HYATT, HYATT DESIGN

STREET OF DREAMS
Watersong

Soaring Views

Colors, materials and furnishings in this glorious home create a refined atmosphere of harmony and balance.

Magnificent landscaping provides a lush Florida-type setting for this outstanding design while stone, bronze and ceramic fountains add more of nature's congenial touches. A beautiful patio beside the front entry displays an inviting pergola and fountain. Inside, in addition to on-site surveillance, state-of-the-art high-speed communication and data wiring prepare the lucky homeowners for the future. From the entry, it's a step down to the living room or dining room. Spectacular interior architecture, including a built-in dining wall, highlights the dining room. Large windows bathe the area with natural light while 24-inch squares of limestone cover the floor.

At the rear of the home, views through the expanse of windows that define the octagonal family room are breathtaking! A customized fireplace and an entertainment center on the opposite wall enhance the gathering possibilities. Two sets of double doors open from the family room to the covered porch—with its summer kitchen—and the lanai beyond. Access to this very livable outdoor area is also granted from the living room and owners suite. Creativity abounds in the breathtakingly beautiful music conservatory and imagination room, which is a step down from the family room. Soaring ceilings, cherry wood floors, fine wood molding and tall windows augment this room's splendor. The view through the trio of arched windows is spectacular day or night.

The family's gourmet cook will enjoy the richness of the kitchen cabinetry with stone and countertop details. A complete

The octagonal family room is the hub of this remarkable home, with access to the covered porch, imagination room, kitchen and breakfast nook.

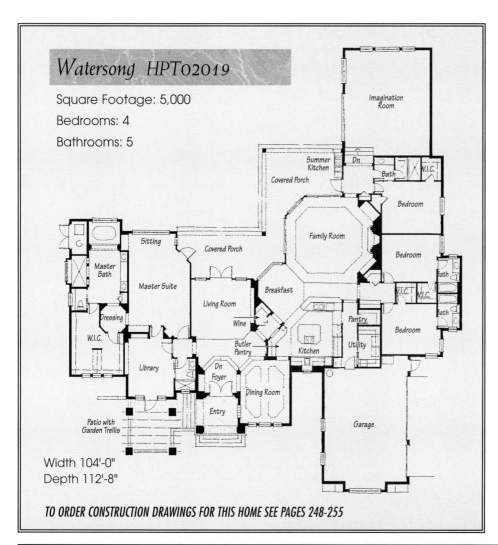

Watersong HPT02019

Square Footage: 5,000
Bedrooms: 4
Bathrooms: 5

Imagination Room

Summer Kitchen

Dn

Bath

W.I.C.

Covered Porch

Bedroom

Sitting

Family Room

Covered Porch

Bedroom

Bath

Master Bath

Master Suite

Breakfast

W.I.C.

W.I.C.

Living Room

Dressing

Wine

Pantry

Bath

W.I.C.

Butler Pantry

Kitchen

Utility

Bedroom

Library

Dn
Foyer

Dining Room

Entry

Garage

Patio with
Garden Trellis

Width 104'-0"
Depth 112'-8"

TO ORDER CONSTRUCTION DRAWINGS FOR THIS HOME SEE PAGES 248-255

line of appliances and a walk-in pantry match the practicality of this room to its beauty. Less formal dining will always be a pleasure in the breakfast nook. Here you can sip your morning coffee while gazing out over the lanai to the lake beyond. Adjacent to the kitchen is the wine vault that includes space for a serious collection of spirits.

On the opposite side of the plan, the owners suite boasts magnificent views. More than a sleeping chamber, this suite includes a spacious sitting room. A

Furnished with a grand piano and Harley Davidson motorcycles, the imagination room is the place where dreams become reality.

small dressing room connects to the private bath and walk-in closet, which features customized shelving and enough space to house the wardrobe of a Hollywood legend. Highlights of the private bath are a whirlpool tub surrounded by columns, a fireplace and wood paneling.

At the front of the plan, the library is accented with handcrafted wood molding. With a full bath nearby and a private door through the pergola at the front of the house, the library would serve well as a home office. Privacy is emphasized in the three family bedrooms on the right side of the home. Each bedroom includes a walk-in closet, and two have private baths. The third bedroom accesses the hall bath outside the imagination room.

DESIGNER: © Greg Hyatt, Hyatt Design, Orlando, Florida
BUILDER: Southpoint Homes
INTERIOR DESIGN: Design Specifications, Inc.
PHOTOGRAPHS: © Visual Solutions Co.

This home, as shown in the photographs, may differ from the actual blueprints. For more detailed information, please check the floor plans carefully.

The arched-window theme throughout the home is evident in the dining-room window and echoed in the graceful architectural lines of the art niche.

Window walls in the family room offer expansive views of the lanai, pool, lake and skylight.

SOFIA

DESIGN BY McDOWELL & ASSOCIATES, INC.

Spa-Like Luxury

The clean lines of smooth-coat stucco embellished with natural Rundle Stone only hint at the richness within.

Wrought-iron spindles and elegant wood railings enclose the grand central stairway, which leads to the lower floor. Ten-foot-high walls and oversized arched passageways announce the central great room, where a breathtaking maple mantel and hood surround the warming fireplace. A centered picture window overlooks the deck and provides more outdoor views. Hardwood flooring and a soaring gothic, domed ceiling lend formality to this magnificent room.

This home, as shown in the photographs, may differ from the actual blueprints. For more detailed information, please check the floor plans carefully.

Adjacent to the great room is the maple kitchen. Hand-built, antique-finished maple cabinetry is coupled with distinctive faux-finished open rafters to foster a warm country atmosphere. Masonry inspired walls and a rustic island increase the charm of this spacious kitchen. Appliances are behind panels for an uncluttered look and to show off the lustrous, stained concrete countertops. Harnessed egg pendants, suspended from the vaulted ceiling, provide elegant illumination and complement the décor. The large nook enjoys a custom-designed milled window.

The owners suite features an expanse of windows and deck access. The unique

STREET OF DREAMS
Sofia

spherical bath includes a walk-in closet, dual vanities topped with stained concrete counters and an automated skylight that brightens the bath without compromising privacy. Jewel-box paneling blends with handcrafted bookcases and a lovely fireplace mantle to create a cozy gathering area. A powder room is nearby. Laundry and storage are accommodated in the mudroom, which adjoins the three-car garage and completes the floor.

A fully equipped media room with a wet bar is at the bottom of the grand stairway. The game room is designed for a billiard

An automated skylight highlights the circular owners bath, which displays an intricate pattern of crushed stone in the center of the tile floor.

Opposite: From the bottom of the staircase, the barrel-vaulted entry makes an impression with its polished gold tones and graceful curves framed by square columns.

A railing under a graceful arch, which repeats the arched theme of the foyer, separates the comfortable guest room from the elegant staircase.

table and provides terrace access beneath the rear deck. Health-conscious family members will appreciate the exercise area, which is located near the wet bar for quick refreshment. An exquisite European wine cellar is perfect for holding a vast collection of the finest spirits.

The completely functional home office with a wall of windows is delightful. Wired with 21st-Century fiber optics, this room can serve as a computer center. The remainder of the lower floor is devoted to family sleeping quarters. The entire lower floor has temperatures maintained through a radiant in-floor heating system. With a professionally landscaped yard, Sofia is a true work of art.

DESIGNER: © McDowell & Associates, Inc.,
Calgary, Alberta
BUILDER: Laratta Homes
INTERIOR DESIGN: Sally Healy Design Ltd.
PHOTOGRAPHS: © Visual Solutions Co.

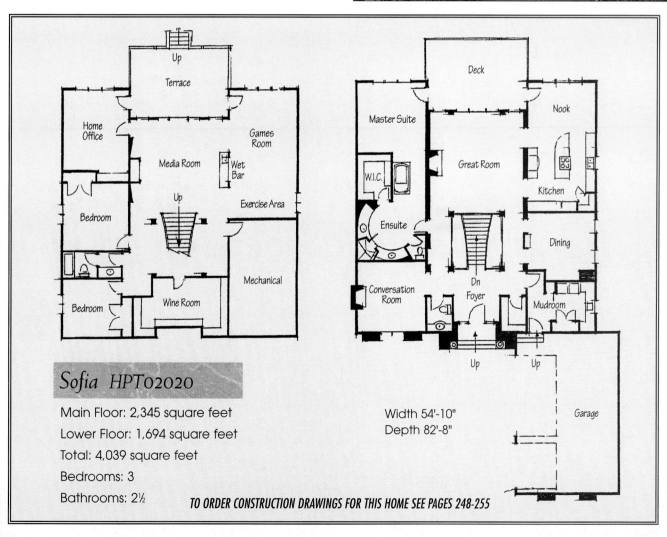

Sofia HPT02020

Main Floor: 2,345 square feet

Lower Floor: 1,694 square feet

Total: 4,039 square feet

Bedrooms: 3

Bathrooms: 2½

Width 54'-10"
Depth 82'-8"

TO ORDER CONSTRUCTION DRAWINGS FOR THIS HOME SEE PAGES 248-255

HAISTENS

DESIGN BY ARCHIVAL DESIGNS, INC.

STREET OF DREAMS
Haistens

Petite Maison

This best-selling plan delivers a high-impact interior rich with architectural accents, inviting amenities and a five-star personality.

This home, as shown in the photographs, may differ from the actual blueprints. For more detailed information, please check the floor plans carefully.

This appealing neoclassical façade, set off by charming multi-pane windows with arched lintels, decorative gabled roofs and two dormer windows, is much more than just a pretty face. French doors flanked by sidelights and framed by square pillars lead to a grand vestibule with a barrel-vaulted ceiling and windows on both sides. The tiled gallery foyer defines the formal rooms with Doric columns, arches and decorative molding. A beam ceiling decorates the study on the right, which includes a fireplace, built-in bookcases, a beautiful hardwood floor and French doors to the front yard. Across the foyer, the dining room features a circular ceiling trim, which frames the chandelier, double doors to the front yard and easy access to the kitchen.

An inviting fireplace in the grand salon welcomes visitors to the back of the home. This magnificent room has a dome ceiling and two sets of lovely French doors that open to the covered brick veranda. Just steps from the formal dining room, the grand salon is a comfortable place for guests to gather—or perhaps they'll want to linger outside on the veranda. Convenient amenities, such as a coat closet and powder room, are thoughtfully placed nearby.

The left wing is dedicated to the family's living space. An open room to the rear of the plan boasts a vaulted ceiling, fireplace and a sliding glass door to the veranda. The gourmet kitchen easily serves the dining room and features a sizable pantry, lots of counter space and a food-prep island with a vegetable sink. A

second island counter with a double sink overlooks the breakfast room, offering a view of the rear property. The cabinet-fronted pantry makes this kitchen a favorite with cooks.

To the right of the plan, an arched entryway leads to a private gallery hall, where double doors open to the owners suite. This rambling retreat includes a spacious bedroom with a beautiful tray ceiling, French doors to the veranda, and a three-sided fireplace shared with a secluded sitting area. A quiet place for the homeowner to relax or read, the sitting room features a vaulted ceiling and sliding doors to the veranda. The lavish bath includes a dual-sink vanity, walk-in closet, separate shower with seat, and a

Decorative columns and graceful arches lead to a spectacular grand salon, which is made cozy by an inviting fireplace and French doors.

Opposite: Guests and family members will linger on the veranda, enjoying gentle breezes, quiet conversation or even stargazing.

An arch-top window brightens the casual living space, including the family room, kitchen and breakfast area.

soaking tub set in a box-bay window. Each of two family bedrooms has its own bath, and one bedroom features a built-in shelf and a walk-in closet.

Stairs off of the grand salon lead to the second-floor's unfinished bonus space. An office with a fireplace and windows overlooking the rear yard, a full bath, a playroom with attic access, and a cedar closet can be developed in the future. Completing the plan is a powder room, laundry room with soaking sink, and a three-car garage with space for a freezer.

DESIGNER: © Archival Designs, Inc.
PHOTOGRAPHS: © Bill Gaddis

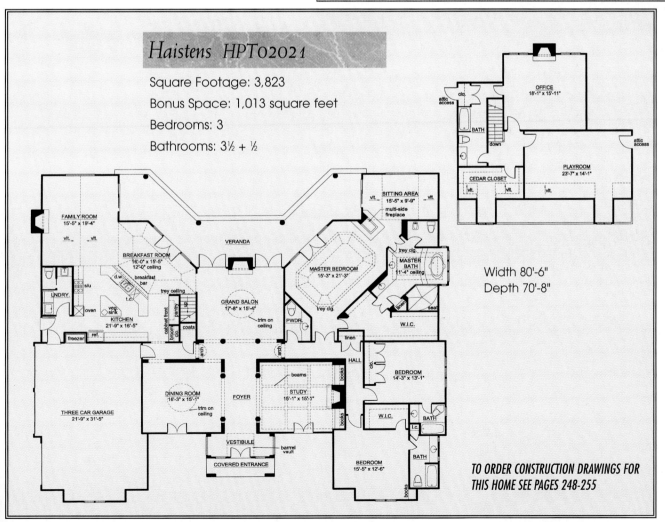

Haistens HPT02021

Square Footage: 3,823

Bonus Space: 1,013 square feet

Bedrooms: 3

Bathrooms: 3½ + ½

Width 80'-6"
Depth 70'-8"

OFFICE
18'-1" x 15'-11"

attic access

clo.

BATH

down

attic access

CEDAR CLOSET

PLAYROOM
23'-7" x 14'-1"

vlt.

FAMILY ROOM
15'-5" x 19'-4"

vlt.

BREAKFAST ROOM
16'-0" x 15'-5"
12'-0" ceiling

breakfast bar

d.w.

LNDRY.

s/u

oven

veg. sink

KITCHEN
21'-9" x 16'-5"

t.c.

freezer

ref.

cabinet front

broom clo.

pantry

coats

trey ceiling

VERANDA

GRAND SALON
17'-8" x 15'-4"

trim on ceiling

arch

SITTING AREA
15'-5" x 9'-9"

multi-side fireplace

vlt.

vlt.

MASTER BEDROOM
15'-3" x 21'-3"

trey clg.

MASTER BATH
11'-4" ceiling

trey clg.

linen

seat

W.I.C.

PWDR.

linen

HALL

clo.

BEDROOM
14'-3" x 13'-1"

THREE CAR GARAGE
21'-9" x 31'-5"

DINING ROOM
16'-3" x 15'-1"

trim on ceiling

FOYER

STUDY
15'-1" x 15'-1"

beams

books

books

W.I.C.

t.c.

BATH

VESTIBULE

barrel vault

COVERED ENTRANCE

BEDROOM
15'-5" x 12'-6"

books

BATH

TO ORDER CONSTRUCTION DRAWINGS FOR THIS HOME SEE PAGES 248-255

La Margaux

Design by Eric S. Brown's *Palladian Design Collection*

STREET OF DREAMS
La Margaux

Young at Heart

With sleek lines and gentle arches, this Mediterranean beauty brings a new brand of dignity and a dash of the past to Sun Country style.

A host of stately columns lends definition to the façade and announces a dazzling interior with well-planned rooms and wide-open spaces. Surrounded by a covered porch, a veranda and a private garden, this lovely home enjoys a bright relationship

This home, as shown in the photographs, may differ from the actual blueprints. For more detailed information, please check the floor plans carefully.

Inset: Decorative columns and a dome ceiling create an aura of elegance in the formal dining room.

with the outdoors. French doors from all of the living areas will invite the beautiful weather inside, along with natural light and gentle breezes. The entry leads to an open foyer and formal parlor, which boasts built-ins and two sets of doors to the veranda. A wet bar and a through-fireplace shared with the study enhances this central area, designed for entertaining as well as quiet family gatherings.

Double doors open from a gallery hall to the secluded study, which could serve as a home office. To the other side of the parlor, an elegant arrangement of columns and arches define the formal dining room, and French doors lead outside. The main section of the veranda invites guests to linger and enjoy conversation, balmy breezes, sunsets and stargazing. The gourmet kitchen serves an eating bar and morning nook and includes the culinary artist's favorite amenities: a walk-in pantry, food-prep island, wet bar and wine cellar. The breakfast

nook provides great interior vistas, with a view of the fireplace in the leisure room. Cozy gatherings and informal events will fit perfectly in this comfortable space—an ideal place for warming up or cooling off.

The leisure room leads to an outdoor kitchen and breezeway, which provides access to a cabana bath and two guest suites. One of the suites is a detached guesthouse with

Above: French doors open the living areas to the veranda, spa and pool.

Opposite: A rambling master suite features a private sitting area with a door to the veranda.

Left: Both comfortable and elegant, the parlor leads outdoors to a spacious entertainment terrace.

a bay living room overlooking the rear yard. This inviting retreat provides a bedroom with built-in shelves and access through the living area to the outdoor amenities, including the pool, deck and spa. Guest Suite 2 features a spacious bath with an oversized shower, walk-in closet and storage.

On the opposite side of the plan, a rambling owners suite features two walk-in closets, a dressing area, separate vanities, an oversized shower and a privacy garden. An archway leads from the bedroom to a sitting area that has a wall of glass and leads to the veranda. A vestibule in the owners wing leads to a secondary suite. Built-ins, front-property views and a sizable bath highlight this guest room. With plenty of space for guests as well as family and friends, this sensational home is a place to live in and love forever.

DESIGNER: © Eric S. Brown's
Palladian Design Collection
PHOTOGRAPHS: © Michael Lowry Photography

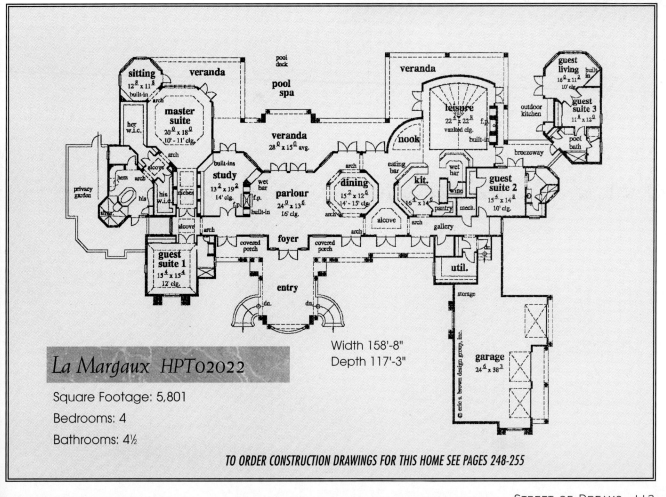

La Margaux HPT02022

Square Footage: 5,801

Bedrooms: 4

Bathrooms: 4½

Width 158'-8"
Depth 117'-3"

TO ORDER CONSTRUCTION DRAWINGS FOR THIS HOME SEE PAGES 248-255

CONCINITAS

DESIGN BY ARCHIVAL DESIGNS, INC.

Open House

An engaging mix of old and new, the ultra-plush interior of this European-style villa calls up the grandeur of times gone by and achieves a look that's just right for today.

Here's a home that pampers the owners as well as guests, with a wide-open casual living area on the first floor and spacious sleeping quarters, a sitting area and an enchanting gallery overlook upstairs. The exterior of this home reverberates with classic touches especially fit for a Mediterranean-style plan. Double-hung windows with decorative lintels, two bold chimneys and a stucco façade distinguish the front elevation. Guests will linger in the grand entry hall, which features a convenient coat closet and storage, and announces a magnificent gallery defined by decorative columns and splendid interior vistas.

An elegant spiral staircase enhances the view and provides access to the second-floor sleeping quarters. The rear of the plan provides a second staircase that's

STREET OF DREAMS
Concinitas

The floor-to-ceiling windows of the grand salon offer plenty of natural light to the interior.

designed to allow hungry family members easy access to the gourmet kitchen and breakfast room. The well-organized kitchen boasts a food-prep island, wrapping counter space, a built-in planning desk and an ample walk-in pantry. A French door and a wall of windows brighten the area, creating an inviting dining space. The breakfast room opens to a splendid keeping room, made both bright and cozy by a fireplace and walls of glass that offer rich views of the back property.

Before dinner, guests will be drawn to the warmth of the fireplace in the grand salon and may continue to enjoy its glow from the formal dining room. An elaborate ceiling treatment and extended-hearth fireplace in the library contribute to a sense of luxury, while an

Fine details create an inviting and elegant environment in the formal dining room.

Opposite: A sitting area in the owners suite is a fine place to enjoy a good book.

The game room sports a vaulted ceiling enhanced by exquisite decorative columns.

aura of spaciousness prevails in the two-story grand salon. The dining hall includes two sets of French doors that open to a terrace with an arbor above—perfect for outdoor dining.

With spacious rooms and lavish amenities, the owners wing is a fabulous retreat that offers kick-off-your-shoes comfort. A two-way fireplace warms the owners bedroom and a private sitting area that's crowned with a tray ceiling. The spacious bath provides a centered whirlpool tub and oversized shower, surrounded on three sides by a vanity and two lavatories. The suite includes separate dressing areas, walk-in closets and toilet compartments—one with a bidet.

DESIGNER: © Archival Designs, Inc.
INTERIOR DESIGN: Bonnie White Interiors
PHOTOGRAPHS: © Bonnie White Interiors

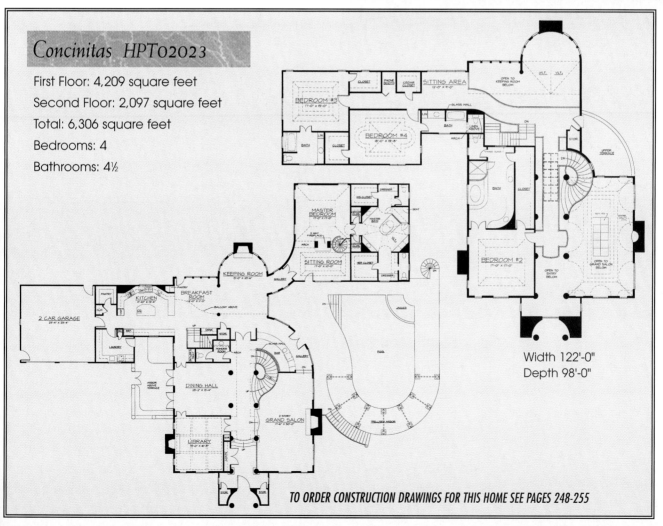

Concinitas HPT02023

First Floor: 4,209 square feet

Second Floor: 2,097 square feet

Total: 6,306 square feet

Bedrooms: 4

Bathrooms: 4½

Width 122'-0"
Depth 98'-0"

TO ORDER CONSTRUCTION DRAWINGS FOR THIS HOME SEE PAGES 248-255

SUMMER NIGHT

DESIGN BY LUCIA CUSTOM HOME DESIGNERS, INC.

Cultural Influences

Creative design and innovative materials come together in an artful composition of comfort and luxury in this European-flavored style.

This charming and imaginative design features a stately stucco exterior with a tile roof and grand inviting entry. Tennessee flagstone covers the entry steps. An arch-top mahogany door with a beveled-glass insert and matching side panels welcomes guests and announces a well-planned interior. The fireplace wall in the living room features ornate woodwork with arched niches and a custom-designed mirror. Built-ins with accent lighting create a cozy yet elegant atmosphere. Lovely French doors

A window brightens the morning nook and the kitchen.

open to the rear covered porch and offer expansive views of the pool area. To the right of the foyer, a secluded library has a lovely triple-window view of the front property.

Comfortably serving up to ten guests, the formal dining room provides a twelve-foot-high ceiling bordered with crown molding. Colorful hand painting highlights a chandelier centered on a plaster medallion detail. Open to the foyer, this room is partially defined by a fluted Tuscan column, which also serves to enhance the space with a formal detail. This exquisite setting leads to the gourmet kitchen through a privacy door. A cooktop island counter and walk-in pantry highlight the well-organized kitchen. A powder room is thoughtfully placed nearby.

Bright colors and accent lighting enliven the gourmet kitchen, which is equipped for entertaining.

Opposite: A finely detailed balustrade lines the elegant stairway, overlooking the living room.

Opposite Inset: The owners suite provides a spacious sitting area that leads outdoors to the rear balcony.

This home, as shown in the photographs, may differ from the actual blueprints. For more detailed information, please check the floor plans carefully.

To the rear of the plan, casual living space accommodates family gatherings—grand or cozy—with a wet bar, built-ins, wide open views and access to the rear covered porch. Here, an outdoor kitchen and convenient powder room provide an invitation to entertain outside. Double doors open to this area from a sizable game room that offers space for a billiard table, media center or even computer equipment.

A side stairway leads to the kitchen from the secondary sleeping quarters, creating easy access for hungry family members. Bedroom 2 has an adjoining playroom, walk-in closet, oversized shower and a tub with a window. Double doors lead from this bedroom out to a large balcony, while a convenient vestibule opens to an exercise room. A hall connects this bedroom suite with an upstairs laundry and with Bedroom 3, which has its own bath and a walk-in closet.

The gallery hall features a balcony overlook to the living room and a door to a second-floor balcony that tops the front entry. An elaborate owners suite boasts a room-sized walk-in closet with a window, a lavish bath and a private sitting area that leads out to the rear balcony. Compartmented toilets and separate vanities provide both convenience and luxury for the owners. On the opposite side of the second floor, a sizable bonus room with a full bath and walk-in closet can be developed into a recreation room or even a guest suite.

DESIGNER: © Lucia Custom Home Designers, Inc.
PHOTOGRAPHS: © Everett & Soulé

Opposite: Stone steps, walkways and a grand terrace add to the beauty of the pool area.

A knee-space vanity and a corner whirlpool tub highlight the owners bath.

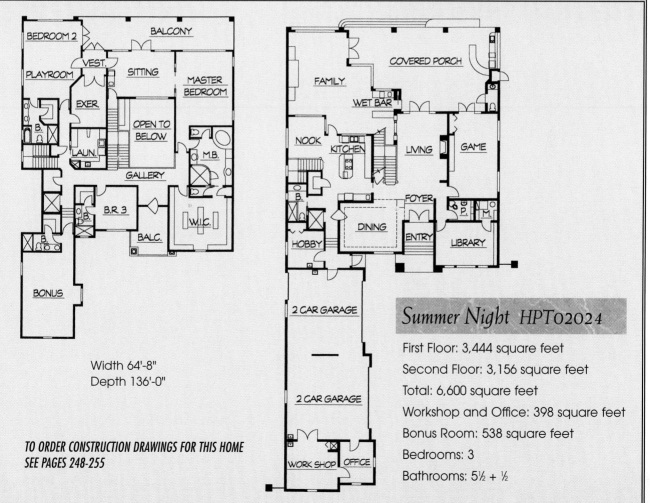

Width 64'-8"
Depth 136'-0"

**TO ORDER CONSTRUCTION DRAWINGS FOR THIS HOME
SEE PAGES 248-255**

BEDROOM 2
BALCONY
PLAYROOM
VEST.
SITTING
MASTER BEDROOM
EXER
OPEN TO BELOW
LAUN.
M.B.
GALLERY
B.R. 3
W.I.C.
BALC.
BONUS

FAMILY
COVERED PORCH
WET BAR
NOOK
KITCHEN
LIVING
GAME
FOYER
DINING
ENTRY
LIBRARY
HOBBY
2 CAR GARAGE
2 CAR GARAGE
WORK SHOP
OFFICE

Summer Night HPT02024

First Floor: 3,444 square feet

Second Floor: 3,156 square feet

Total: 6,600 square feet

Workshop and Office: 398 square feet

Bonus Room: 538 square feet

Bedrooms: 3

Bathrooms: 5½ + ½

VILLA TOSCANA

DESIGN BY ERIC S. BROWN'S *PALLADIAN DESIGN COLLECTION*

Outside In

A stunning interpretation of Mediterranean style, this home declares its independence with walls of windows that bring in the light and a sense of the outdoors.

The sprawling footprint of this gorgeous home begins with a gated entry that leads up then down to a grand courtyard, replete with amenities that invite gatherings. A footbridge allows guests to walk over the monumental pool, which features a spa

STREET OF DREAMS
Villa Toscana

This home, as shown in the photographs, may differ from the actual blueprints.
For more detailed information, please check the floor plans carefully.

A guest suite with a private sitting room opens to the pool and spa.

and a beverage counter served by the outdoor kitchen. A generous courtyard and deck surround the pool. Steps lead up to the grand entry, where double doors provide a spectacular welcome to a well-planned interior. The courtyard pool, landscape and covered veranda extend the home's living space outdoors while creating views from every room.

Two walls of windows brighten the central parlor, which boasts a massive fireplace, built-ins and sliding-glass-door access to the veranda. An alcove with a wet bar that offers a pass-through to the sitting area of the veranda softly transitions the formal to informal space, making this the perfect home for entertaining on any scale. Nearby, a convenient powder room maintains privacy for the owners suite.

A gallery hall that opens from the front veranda provides double doors to the owners retreat—a sumptuous suite with a large dressing area, two walk-in closets, separate vanities, a compartmented toilet and bidet,

and a garden tub. The bath opens to an exercise room, which allows additional storage and access from the veranda. This opulent wing has views to both the courtyard and the rear property, and the bath looks out to a private tropical garden.

Nearby, a vestibule with a curiosity niche provides access to the octagonal library. Four tall windows brighten this quiet room, crowned by a tray ceiling. This wing includes a guest suite with its own sitting

Elaborate details decorate the vaulted ceiling of the formal dining room.

Opposite: Great views and plenty of natural light brighten the stately library.

Retreating walls of glass provide wide views throughout the home.

area, built-ins, private bath and extra storage. Double doors lead from the sitting room to a private area of the front veranda, pool and spa.

Casual living space includes an open leisure room with an entertainment center and a two-sided fireplace shared with the formal dining room. Wide views and a vaulted dome ceiling create an elegant place that's just right for traditional events as well as informal gatherings. A butler's pantry facilitates planned occasions and leads to the kitchen, which features a center cooktop island.

DESIGNER: © Eric S. Brown's
Palladian Design Collection
PHOTOGRAPHS: © Laurence Taylor Architectural Photography

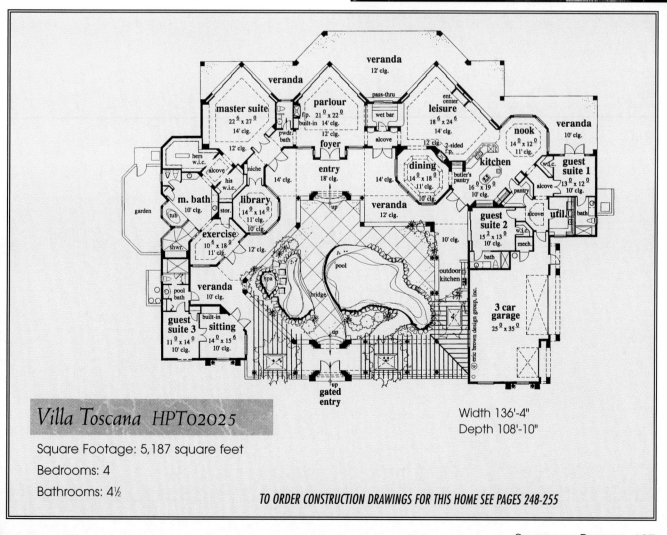

Villa Toscana HPT02025

Square Footage: 5,187 square feet
Bedrooms: 4
Bathrooms: 4½

Width 136'-4"
Depth 108'-10"

TO ORDER CONSTRUCTION DRAWINGS FOR THIS HOME SEE PAGES 248-255

OSPREY

DESIGN BY LUCIA CUSTOM HOME DESIGNERS, INC.

STREET OF DREAMS
Osprey

Chic and Simple

A tantalizing blend of Spanish Colonial and contemporary styles, this singular design lays claim to a wealth of views and a stunning interior that's ready for the future.

Designed for waterfront living, this sensational home combines elements of the past with an array of imaginative amenities designed to carry through to tomorrow's lifestyles. All of the major rooms enjoy wide views oriented to the rear of the site, which boasts a lake with a contemplative fountain. This property also includes a pool and spa, surrounded by a beam-and-column system that enhances the area, allowing a spectacular rear perspective from the lake.

The foyer opens to the living room, a grand two-story space that incorporates a tasteful architecture with details such as columns, arches and intricate ceiling details. A focal-point fireplace warms the room and provides an engaging complement to the built-in bookshelves and clerestory windows. This room opens to a gallery hall with twin sets of doors that open to a gorgeous lanai. To the right of the foyer, a convenient powder room and a coat closet frame the entrance to a secluded and stunning study. A gently curved wall of windows brings in views and a sense of nature to this comfortable room.

Just off the foyer, the formal dining room features a lovely triple-window view of the front grounds and French doors that open to a secluded courtyard. A privacy door leads to the well-planned kitchen. This culinary paradise provides precision appliances, a food-prep island counter, double sink, wrapping counter space and plenty of custom-designed cabinetry. The center island provides a built-in granite table for informal dining. Surrounded by a bay window, this casual eating area overlooks the lanai and enjoys lots of early morning light. Nearby, a walk-in pantry and wet bar help serve planned events.

The owners suite boasts two walk-in closets, a dressing area and a morning kitchen that's near the door to the lanai—a perfect place for coffee and orange juice. The bedroom provides wide views through a lovely bay window. An

Inset: The elegant dining room opens to a quiet courtyard.

Opposite: The gourmet kitchen takes in stunning views.

Below: Interior details abound in the grand central living room.

OSPREY

The owners suite includes a spacious sitting area and a bay window.

Opposite: A beautiful step-up whirlpool tub highlights the owners bath.

The study boasts a stunning wall of glass.

angled whirlpool tub highlights the owners bath, which includes a separate walk-in shower. Two vanity areas, plenty of linen storage and a compartmented toilet and bidet complete this dazzling retreat.

On the opposite side of the plan, a hall leads to a sizable laundry room with plenty of built-ins. Secluded to the rear of the home, a secondary bedroom has a walk-in closet and access to a full bath. A double window brings in daylight and a door leads out to a spacious patio with an outdoor kitchen. The family room and guest bath also open to the covered patio, which is carefully defined by beautiful square columns.

Cutting-edge architecture allows vaulted interior vistas and gallery views of the formal rooms from the second floor. Each of the three bedrooms on this floor has a private full bath and walk-in closet. A gallery hall connects the suites to a spacious bonus room with a wet bar, tower windows and access to the front balcony. At the other end of the hall, a door leads out to a rear balcony. With plenty of overlooks, wide views, flex space and room for guests, this extremely livable level offers a sublime complement to the luxury and comfort of the main floor.

DESIGNER: © Lucia Custom Home Designers, Inc.
PHOTOGRAPHS: © Everett & Soulé

This home, as shown in the photographs, may differ from the actual blueprints. For more detailed information, please check the floor plans carefully.

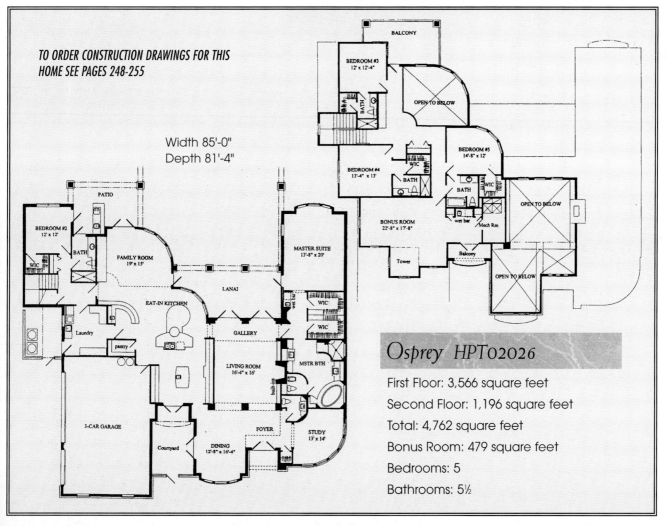

TO ORDER CONSTRUCTION DRAWINGS FOR THIS HOME SEE PAGES 248-255

Width 85'-0"
Depth 81'-4"

Osprey HPT02026

First Floor: 3,566 square feet
Second Floor: 1,196 square feet
Total: 4,762 square feet
Bonus Room: 479 square feet
Bedrooms: 5
Bathrooms: 5½

THE WESTPORT

DESIGN BY DONALD J. FUGINA, JR., DONALD JOSEPH, INC.

Lakeside Luxury

Panoramic lake views are provided throughout this stunning dream home.

Striking inside and out, this contemporary design has a heartwarming disposition. Near the entry, a contemporary turret, enhanced with tall windows, houses an impressive spiral staircase, which is accented with a decorative balustrade of wrought iron and plaster. The foyer's teak hardwood floors and throughway to the patio preview the opulence of the interior. The open floor plan is immediately apparent with the living and dining areas on each side of the foyer, defined by decorative columns. The living room features a fireplace with a special mantel of wood, stone

The rear of this dream house is dedicated to informal family living, with a kitchen, nook, theater room and family room. The modified U-shaped kitchen includes granite-slab countertops, commercial-grade appliances and lovely hardwood floors. A matching island separates the kitchen from the breakfast nook. Thematic iron lighting fixtures add elegance to the theater room, where guests and family members will enjoy favorite movies and shows on an overhead-projection theater system. The wonderful wine vault adjoining the theater room is more than just a niche—it has a 3,000-bottle capacity and central cooling for added security.

Ideal for viewing the lake, the family room brings nature inside through wraparound windows and double glass doors. Outside, a wide entertainment terrace hosts a built-in barbecue and a serving center.

STREET OF DREAMS
The Westport

Curving up from the foyer, the grand stairway leads to a gallery hall and sleeping quarters.

and plaster. Custom-built niches on both sides of the fireplace display *objets d'art*.

Double doors connect the dining room and the kitchen, while a hallway leads to the powder room. A breathtaking *trompe l'oeil* gives the illusion of an outdoor walkway. A study with a box-beamed ceiling is located at the end of the hallway.

Even on cold days, the patio remains warm, thanks to the built-in natural gas heater. A second spiral stairway rises on the terrace for access to the sweeping balcony surrounding the owners suite.

On the second floor, a gallery leads from the top of the grand stairway to the owners suite and a wide covered balcony. Abundant amenities in this suite include a warming fireplace, a second *trompe l'oeil*, thematic lighting and a curved wall of glass. Stargazing from the whirlpool tub is no problem because it faces the balcony's glass wall. This private bath includes a room-sized walk-in closet and a dual-head shower. A smaller balcony over the main entry of the home is accessed from the gallery. One secondary bedroom is equipped with a generous walk-in closet and private full bath. Another secondary bedroom has a walk-in closet. A full bath is

The kitchen's polished look is achieved with granite slab counter-tops and a pre-fin-ished teak hardwood floor.

Opposite: With a fabu-lous built-in barbecue and a natural gas patio heater, the entertainment terrace is rarely off-limits at party time.

Reflected in the mirror of the powder room is a trompe l'oeil.

nearby. The laundry room is conveniently located on this floor. Window coverings have been custom designed to harmonize with each room's architectural theme. A three-car garage completes the plan.

DESIGNER: © Donald J. Fugina, Jr.,
Donald Joseph, Inc.,
Sacramento, California
BUILDER: Houseworks, Inc.
INTERIOR DESIGN: Donald J. Fugina Jr.,
and Karen Messing,
Donald Joseph, Inc.
PHOTOGRAPHS: © Visual Solutions Co.

This home, as shown in the photographs, may differ from the actual blueprints. For more detailed information, please check the floor plans carefully.

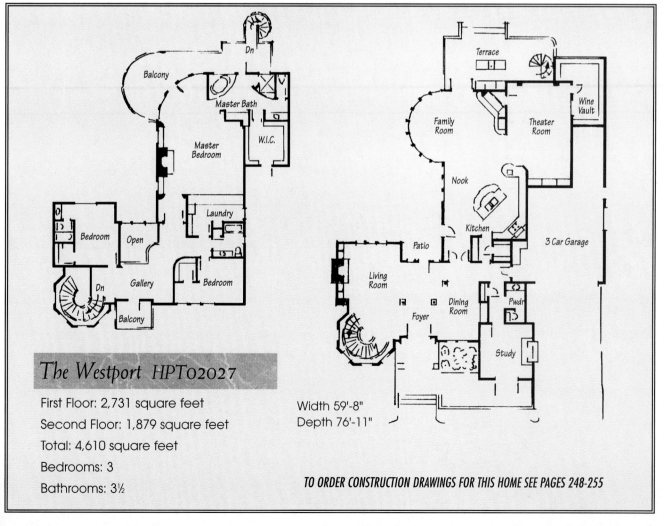

The Westport HPT02027

First Floor: 2,731 square feet

Second Floor: 1,879 square feet

Total: 4,610 square feet

Bedrooms: 3

Bathrooms: 3½

Width 59'-8"
Depth 76'-11"

TO ORDER CONSTRUCTION DRAWINGS FOR THIS HOME SEE PAGES 248-255

VILLA UDINÉ

DESIGN BY AMERICAN DESIGN CONSULTANTS, INC.

Natural Beauty

A thoughtful mix of contemporary and eclectic styles, the distinguished architecture of this desert villa breathes with a comfortable elegance.

Not far from Tucson, Arizona, the historical setting of the Estates at Honeybee Ridge provides wide city views and invites a new appreciation of incredible sunsets. Villa Udiné was created to show harmony in a natural surrounding with the implementation of modern materials. The Spanish-tile accents, stucco façade and varying roof heights give this home the feel of a pueblo. The sleek lines and low profile seem to grow out of the culture-rich land, with a classic yet cutting-edge appearance that's timeless, native and absolutely genuine.

The entry foyer features inlaid tumbled-marble mosaic flooring and a view that extends through to the pool, fountain and covered trellis of the rear property. A sixteen-foot ceiling in the great room enhances the interior vista from the elegant entry, while original art, beautifully coordinated wool area rugs and dramatic faux-finished walls create a finished look.

A corner fireplace, built-in bookshelves and cabinetry, and sliding glass doors provide definition to the open arrangement of the formal rooms. The dining room leads to a fabulous kitchen through a well-equipped butler's pantry. Guests will linger in the Arizona room, whatever the weather. With its own fireplace and panoramic views of the luxuri-

STREET OF DREAMS
Villa Udine

Classic lines define the covered trellis, highlighting the pool and spa.

The living room provides a corner fireplace and custom-built bookshelves.

Above: A guest bedroom has a lovely corner window and sitting area.

Opposite: Marble accents and inlaid tile enhance the owners suite, which includes a cozy sitting area and hearth.

ous rear grounds, this comfortable space also provides a relaxing retreat for the owners.

The homeowners sitting area opens from the Arizona room and provides a third fireplace for the design. This cozy corner will inspire great novels, or at least allow a quiet space to read one—and give the busy owners a little well-deserved privacy. The bedroom includes a wall of built-in shelves and access to a private outdoor area. A lavish bath in this suite features accent marble and inlaid tile. A double walk-in closet has a garment cabinet system. French doors lead from the owners suite to a secluded den, which has its own access to a hall bath.

On the opposite side of the plan, each of two secondary bedrooms has a private bath and walk-in closet. A gallery hall leads to the kitchen and breakfast area. Double doors open from the casual dining space to an L-shaped patio—an inviting place to enjoy morning coffee. A guest suite provides its own entry and boasts a lavish bath with an instant-steam shower. A four-car garage with service for an electric car completes the plan.

DESIGNER: © American Design Consultants, Inc., Tucson, Arizona
BUILDER: Louis Marson & Sons
INTERIOR DESIGN: Contents/Techline
PHOTOGRAPHS: © Visual Solutions Co.

Villa Udiné HPT02028

Square Footage: 5,200 square feet
Bedrooms: 4
Bathrooms: 4½

Width 108'-0"
Depth 112'-6"

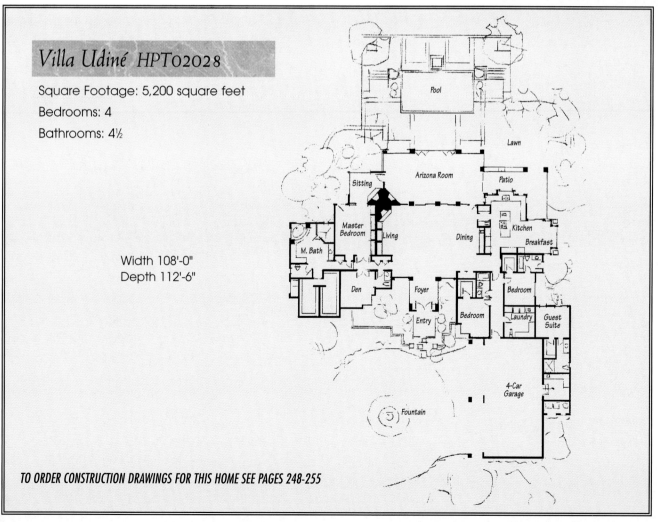

TO ORDER CONSTRUCTION DRAWINGS FOR THIS HOME SEE PAGES 248-255

THE VENETIAN

DESIGN BY JAMES E. GILGENBACH, ARCHITECT

Modern European

With a sophisticated look and a heart of gold, this stately design celebrates Old World artisanship and radiates the joy of luxury.

The casual, comfortable ambiance created by melding European style with soft, neutral tones, fine furnishings and cutting-edge amenities sets a new definition of luxury in this beautiful Sun Country home. Expansive walls of windows frame breathtaking views of lavish gardens, while complementing the interior's subtle décor. Plush

A graceful arch framed by spiral-carved columns defines the glorious dining room.

This home, as shown in the photographs, may differ from the actual blueprints. For more detailed information, please check the floor plans carefully.

A custom stone fireplace warms the spacious living room.

Plush furnishings and finely detailed wood honor a timeless design tradition in the family room.

furnishings make an ideal backdrop for any occasion—traditional or informal. Antique accoutrements honor a design tradition that never goes out of style, becoming even more attractive as the gentle patina of everyday living and memorable events leave their mark.

This West Palm Beach residence features hand-carved and finished imported wood furnishings combined with unique wall and window treatments, as well as original artwork from around the world, creating a sophisticated environment for gracious comfortable living. Like a fine painting that reveals more details as one lives with it, this interior provides a depth of detail that becomes more interesting as the home is enjoyed.

The entry leads through mahogany doors that measure a full ten feet in height, adding to the grandeur. Inside, intricate ceiling treatments complement custom woodwork and natural stone floors. To the left of the foyer, which has a marble floor,

fabulous archways and decorative columns exemplifying classic Venetian architecture define the formal dining room. Views of the front property enhance the inviting atmosphere, while a built-in servery provides a facility for handling planned events of any size.

Just steps away from the dining room, the kitchen provides plenty of storage and counter space, including a center food-prep island. Culinary artists will appreciate the high-end, restaurant-quality appliances, walk-in pantry and impressive poolside views. A serving counter overlooks the family room, which features access to a bath shared with a secondary bedroom. A spacious dining area between the family room and kitchen is an ideal place for informal meals.

Above: The dazzling heart of this home is the formal living room.

Custom woodwork complements state-of-the-art wiring in the library, a room that can easily serve as a home office.

The heart of this home is dedicated to the grand living room. Imported furnishings rich with Italian silk and cotton fabrics, unique wall and window treatments, original European art and accessories, and accent niches surround an intricately carved stone fireplace. A wall of glass overlooks the covered patio and pool area, and twin doors provide access to the inviting outdoor retreat. Striking colors and fine woodworks define the nearby library. Built-in cabinetry and 21st-Century wiring make this room easily convertible to a home office, computer center or even a media room.

A set of majestic doors leads to the owners suite, which provides access to the pool, spa and luxurious rear grounds. French doors open from the bedroom and the adjacent exercise room, or study, to a covered patio, where the fortunate owners may choose to enjoy their morning coffee. This secluded retreat

includes a wet bar, or morning kitchen. The owners bath features two walk-in closets that bracket a hall leading to a sumptuous step-up whirlpool tub and separate oversized shower. Fine marble floors and countertops keep treasured Italian traditions alive in this elaborate haven.

Opposite Above: A lavish owners suite opens to a covered patio.

Opposite Below: A sumptuous step-up whirlpool tub sets off the owners bath.

An interior window sets off stunning fixtures in the walk-in shower.

DESIGNER: © James E. Gilgenbach, Architect,
Boca Raton, Florida
BUILDER: ARCH Enterprises, Inc.
INTERIOR DESIGN: Carole Korn Interiors
PHOTOGRAPHS: © Visual Solutions Co.

The Venetian HPT02029

Square Footage: 4,282 square feet

Bedrooms: 4

Bathrooms: 4½

Width 85'-0"
Depth 100'-0"

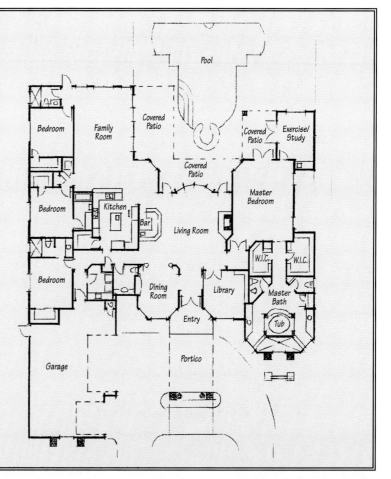

TO ORDER CONSTRUCTION DRAWINGS FOR THIS HOME SEE PAGES 248-255

Postless sliding doors in the family room and formal dining room make it easy to pass between indoor and outdoor living areas.

ASHFORD

DESIGN BY THE SATER DESIGN COLLECTION

Happy Haven

Dressed with crafted touches typically found in much larger homes, this spectacular Sun Country plan is, quite simply, one in a million.

A towering entry flanked by columns and topped by an arch and decorative iron railings greets guests and sets off this sensational façade. Interesting rooflines and plenty of windows enhance a stucco exterior that's a gentle mix of European past and present. The rear grounds include a sprawling lanai, pool and spa. Techno-savvy buyers will appreciate the Ashford's Category-5 wiring, programmable lighting-control systems, web-ready television and distributed video and audio systems.

The spacious living room boasts artful window treatments. The fireplace surround is carved Mexican stone.

This home, as shown in the photographs, may differ from the actual blueprints. For more detailed information, please check the floor plans carefully.

The foyer opens to the living room, which offers wide outdoor vistas through a window wall that juts out onto the veranda. This grand space is made cozy with a fireplace and a surround made of carved Mexican stone. Decorative columns and a magnificent bay window define the formal dining room, which overlooks the front courtyard.

Traditional events can be served through the butler's pantry, a well-equipped service area that leads to the gourmet kitchen. The family cook will enjoy the butcher-block island, food-prep sink, walk-in pantry and cooktop counter with stone surround. Recessed lighting and beautiful natural materials make this kitchen a comfort zone where family and guests will want to gather. A snack bar separates the kitchen from the leisure room and breakfast area. The morning nook boasts wide views of the lanai, which includes a summer kitchen. Built-ins and views of the pool and outdoor fireplace highlight the leisure room, while a mitered window brightens the entire space.

To the left of the foyer, double doors open to a study, brightened by three windows in a bay. Custom built-in cabinetry and a desk create a stately room that easily converts to a home office or computer center. Three transoms bring in plenty of daylight and make this room an inviting place to relax. This room could also be used as a parlor—a secluded place to enjoy quiet conversation.

Double doors open to the owners suite, which features two walk-in closets and a sitting area with its own access to the veranda.

A butcher-block island with a prep sink, commercial-grade appliances and an elegant stone surround for the cooktop typify the level of detail provided by the builder.

Fairways, the pool and a lake are all visible from this lavish retreat. The owners bath boasts natural stone floors, custom cabinets and granite countertops. Amenities include a garden tub, dressing area and separate shower. A private garden on the side of the home offers serene views from the shower and whirlpool tub. An additional full bath with a circular shower off the master foyer doubles as a pool bath or second owners bath.

Two guest suites are thoughtfully placed on the right side of the plan. One of the bedrooms provides a walk-in closet and full bath, while the other includes a bay window and dual-sink vanity.

Closets in both bedrooms are crafted of furniture-grade maple cabinetry.

The three-car garage provides a service entrance that leads to a laundry equipped with a soaking sink, counter space and a built-in ironing board. Great indoor/outdoor living is accomplished in this home through postless sliding glass doors that offer easy access to the veranda and pool from the leisure and family rooms. An expansive lanai covers the outdoor summer kitchen and grill, providing an ideal place for outdoor entertaining. The unique pool, spa, terrace and garden enjoy spectacular views that extend beyond the rear property.

Rich with detailed wood, the study can easily be converted to a library—or even a parlor for quiet conversation.

Opposite: Graceful arches and Doric-style columns define the dining room.

DESIGNER: © The Sater Design Collection
BUILDER: Mark Wilson, London Bay Homes
INTERIOR DESIGN: Romanza Architectural Interiors
PHOTOGRAPHS: © Laurence Taylor

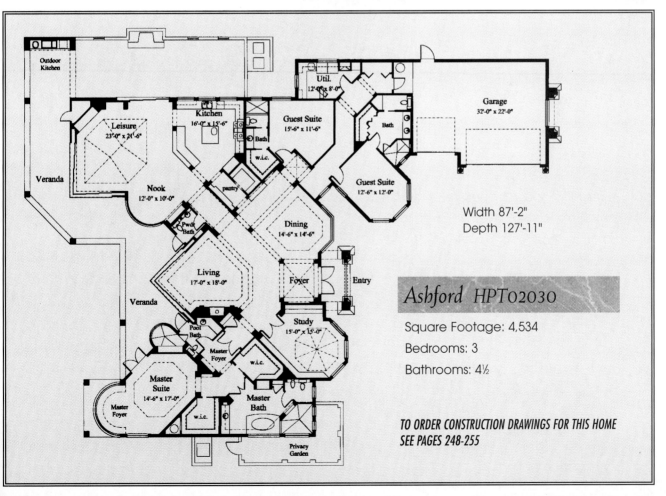

Width 87'-2"
Depth 127'-11"

Ashford HPT02030

Square Footage: 4,534

Bedrooms: 3

Bathrooms: 4½

TO ORDER CONSTRUCTION DRAWINGS FOR THIS HOME
SEE PAGES 248-255

CASA BELLA

DESIGN BY ROSS DESIGN GROUP

Global Economy

With timeless elements borrowed from southern Spain and northern Africa, this waterfront design optimizes the home site, using every square inch to its fullest advantage.

Historic architectural details and timeless materials such as reclaimed wood floors, stained wood beams, stamped tin, plaster frescos, Mexican pavers and painted fretwork allow this unique home to feel as if it were built for a world traveler with eclectic taste. Intricately carved columns support glorious arches and a myriad of rooflines, creating an appealing façade that's just the beginning of a truly spectacular home. Inside, fresco plaster paint techniques highlight two transitional vestibules with lighted dome ceilings. Several custom built-ins with Chippendale mahogany and aged red lacquer with strap hinges add dash from the past. The extensive use of crown molding, wood beams and accent lighting throughout the home creates a rich backdrop for luxurious furnishings, art and accessories.

STREET OF DREAMS
Casa Bella

Custom-built ten-foot-tall cypress entry doors lead to a two-story foyer and hall, which features a grand circular custom staircase with an S-curved top and wood flooring. A see-through masonry fireplace with carved stone surrounds connects the parlor with the formal dining room. Twin sets of lovely French doors lead out to the lanai from the parlor, while the dining room provides its own access to the outdoors.

A magnificent study, home office or den provides customized wood cabinetry with built-in computer and television space. A fanlight crowns a wood window that allows plenty of daylight inside. This home features a customized home electronic system that includes surround sound, stereo speakers, multi-zone remote controlling, digital satellite cabling, high-grade telephone/data cabling, state-of-the-art home automation, a security system and video monitoring.

An exquisite game room provides a unique custom built-in entertainment console with surround sound and multi-zone remote controlling.

The spacious family room has an interior vista of the gourmet kitchen, with a marble-topped center island and a tiled range hood supported by carved elephant brackets.

The parlor features a see-through masonry fireplace with a custom-carved stone surround.

The formal dining room features stunning hardwood floors and a beautiful fresco. Nearby, custom-built cypress doors open to a wine room that displays well-organized cedar wine racks with a tasting table, beam ceiling and stucco walls. A butler's pantry leads from the dining room to the custom-tiled kitchen. Furniture-quality cabinetry in a distressed walnut finish with a marble-topped center island in a soft ebony finish complement a variety of tile details, including broken mosaics, one-inch glass tiles and rustic stone patterning. A wide window brightens the spacious breakfast area.

A variety of custom tile details include a fresco plaster paint technique, found in a transitional vestibule with a lighted dome ceiling.

Opposite: A trio of arch-top windows brightens the family room and complements the use of reclaimed beams and crown molding.

Furniture-quality cabinetry in a distressed walnut finish complements a center island with a soft ebony finish.

Views of the lake provide a rich backdrop for the plush furnishings of the formal dining room, enhanced by honey-hued hardwood floors.

Philippine shell panels cradle an elegant whirlpool tub in the owners private bath.

Upstairs, a balcony extends the game room over the parlor below. A unique built-in audio/visual console and wet bar with an under-the-counter refrigerator create an inviting leisure space for the family. The upper hallway leads to the secondary bedroom suites. Each of these two rooms has a full bath and walk-in closet. A privacy door at the end of the hall protects the sleeping quarters from the sounds of the open game room.

The owners bedroom features a private sitting room and custom-built cabinetry.

Warm weather is a key component of any villa and outdoor living is part and parcel of the lifestyle. The extensive landscape package includes a terraced interlocking split-block wall surrounding the pool area. The pool features a vanishing waterline and separate spa. A detached patio provides a barbecue for outdoor cooking. A stone paver motor court leads to a four-car garage.

DESIGNER: © Ross Design Group, Orlando, Florida
BUILDER: Booher Development Corporation
INTERIOR DESIGN: Marc-Michaels Interior Design, Inc.
PHOTOGRAPHS: © Laurence Taylor

A lavish guest suite provides the kind of style and comfort that will make a visitor want to extend her or his stay.

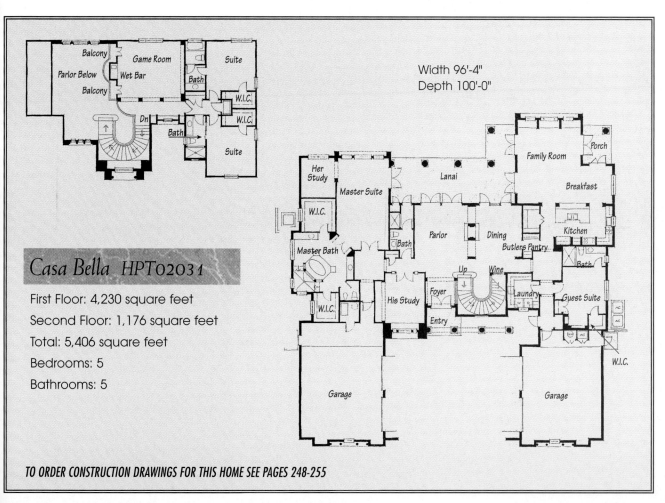

Width 96'-4"
Depth 100'-0"

Casa Bella HPT02031

First Floor: 4,230 square feet

Second Floor: 1,176 square feet

Total: 5,406 square feet

Bedrooms: 5

Bathrooms: 5

TO ORDER CONSTRUCTION DRAWINGS FOR THIS HOME SEE PAGES 248-255

EL PARAISO

DESIGN BY MARK A. CORSON

Heaven on Earth

This private paradise achieves its casual Euro-Caribbean character by mixing Spanish, English and French influences and creating an environment that invites joy, tranquility and happiness.

Tall windows wrap this Euro-Caribbean exterior with dazzling details and allow plenty of natural light to fill the rooms. The vision of the builder, JAT Homes, was to create an atmosphere that feels like paradise, with high style and special features that add beauty and function to this fabulous design. The raised foyer provides a magnificent

A massive stone fireplace flanked by decorative art niches serves as a focal point in the living room.

This home, as shown in the photographs, may differ from the actual blueprints. For more detailed information, please check the floor plans carefully.

Graceful arched windows and a dramatic chandelier highlight the formal dining room.

view through the living room, where a twelve-foot glass wall allows the vista to extend to the pool enclave, lake and golf course. An extraordinary stone fireplace flanked by decorative art niches highlights the living room. A few steps away, the formal dining room integrates graceful arch-top windows, a dramatic chandelier and wood-inlay flooring with a stone border, creating an inviting setting for any occasion. The European kitchen is equipped to serve every event, traditional or casual, and provides 21st-Century amenities and spectacular views. State-of-the-art appliances, granite countertops, a walk-in pantry and freestanding center island with cooktop will spoil the culinary artist.

A spacious kitchen with state-of-the-art appliances, granite countertops and an island cooktop opens to the formal rooms and the casual living areas.

The raised entry overlooks the foyer and living room and enjoys a wide view of the stunning pool enclave.

An open arrangement of the casual living space encourages conversation in the family room and breakfast area, and allows the family cook to participate. Windows line the octagonal breakfast nook and brighten the entire area. A door leads out to a covered patio, a summer kitchen with built-in grill, and a cabana bath. Access to the bath is also provided through the family room.

Comfortable, cozy and high-tech describes the media/game room. This 390-square-foot space houses a home theater or media room that provides plush seating for up to eight people. An audio center and built-in bar achieve the perfect entertainment area. French doors open to a private patio and to a brick walkway that leads to the pool and spa.

The owners wing provides a private hall that includes a powder room with stone-and-slate flooring, a custom-framed mirror and sconces that preside over custom cabinetry. Nearby, a vestibule opens to a gazebo-shaped den with tall windows that allow plenty of daylight. Double doors open from the vestibule to a sumptuous exercise/massage room.

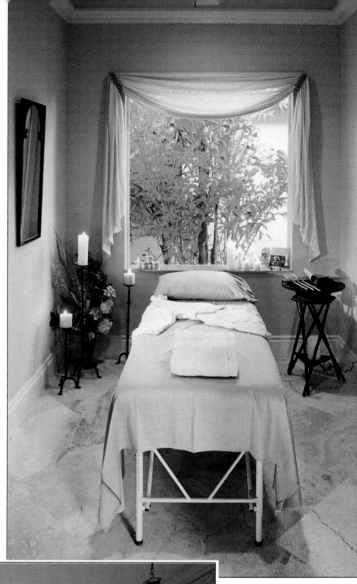

A unique aromatherapy and massage room complements the owners bath.

The owners suite features a sunken tub and offers serene views of the plush surroundings.

Floor-to-ceiling windows in the owners suite offer spectacular views of the pool, water and golf fairway.

The owners bedroom suite provides a sensational view of the pool and golf fairway through floor-to-ceiling glass. A sitting area leads outdoors to the spa and a secluded area of the sizable pool. Two walk-in closets bracket a dressing area that leads to the lavish bath. Intricate stone flooring surrounds a sunken whirlpool tub, oversized shower, double-bowl vanity and compartmented toilet.

A service entrance on the opposite side of the plan leads to a laundry and a quiet guest suite. This spacious bedroom and private bath could easily accommodate a live-in relative. Nearby, a family bedroom has a walk-in closet and its own full bath with a tub and shower. The three-car garage adjoins a separate golf-cart space with an entrance from the motor court fountain area.

DESIGNER: © Mark A. Corson,
Jensen Beach, Florida
BUILDER: JAT Homes
INTERIOR DESIGN: a'Vare Design Group
PHOTOGRAPHS: © Visual Solutions Co.

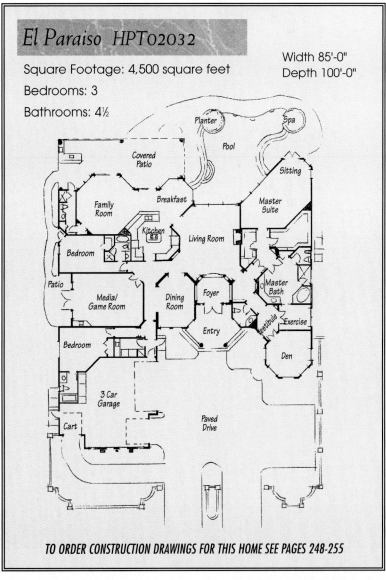

El Paraiso HPT02032

Square Footage: 4,500 square feet
Bedrooms: 3
Bathrooms: 4½

Width 85'-0"
Depth 100'-0"

TO ORDER CONSTRUCTION DRAWINGS FOR THIS HOME SEE PAGES 248-255

ATRAYENTE

DESIGN BY MICHAEL G. ALMLI CONSTRUCTION COMPANY, INC.

New Balance

An inviting mix of exquisite textiles, soothing colors and natural wood creates a Southwestern atmosphere that draws a fine line between home and nature.

Atrayente is filled with beautiful artwork, furniture and rugs, all selected to enhance the color scheme found in a natural desert setting. The interior furnishings and land-

STREET OF DREAMS
Atrayente

scape design of this spacious home celebrates contemporary Sonoran-style living and seamlessly embodies nature's comfort and ease. The extensive use of wood treatments, inviting porches and idyllic courtyards achieves a superb balance between indoor and outdoor living. Authentic wire-brushed interior and exterior cedar doors and moldings complement a warm and interesting mix of contemporary, Native American, European, Asian, African and Mexican accoutrements.

Flagstone flooring and a beautiful beehive fireplace highlight the rear patio.

This home, as shown in the photographs, may differ from the actual blueprints. For more detailed information, please check the floor plans carefully.

The living-room design integrates a soft color palette with views of the serene desert setting.

ATRAYENTE

A classic Southwestern stucco façade, private courtyard and fountain announce this striking design. A wonderful flagstone-and-brick walkway leads to the cedar-door entry and wide-open foyer, which separates the formal rooms. Rustic wood trim surrounds the entry, while Satillo tile floors enhance the Sonoran atmosphere throughout the home.

The sumptuous use of wool, linen and cashmere complements a sleek stone fireplace framed by views in the sitting area of the owners suite.

Lamps hand-made from stone, wood and ceramics harmonize with a hand-carved canterra stone fireplace.

Even formal meals take on the ease and comfort of this region in a stunning, open dining room. Three large windows display gorgeous outdoor views and bring in plenty of daylight as well as the natural beauty of the desert. Hand-fitted wallcoverings and matching window treatments harmonize with area rugs in the dining and living rooms.

Solid granite slab countertops and custom-designed alder-wood cabinetry adorn the kitchen. One-of-a-kind, hand-burnished copper counters, and a custom backsplash and hood highlight the kitchen and bar. High-intensity, low-voltage lighting shines on state-of-the-art appliances. A central island adds storage space and a snack counter, while an informal eating area fills a stylish bay, which overlooks the rear porch.

A hand-carved, custom-designed canterra stone fireplace warms the family room, while the adjoining entertainment area provides access to the rear porch. Flagstone flooring and a beautiful beehive fireplace create an inviting

Atrayente HPT02033

Square Footage: 3,640

Bedrooms: 4

Bathrooms: 3½

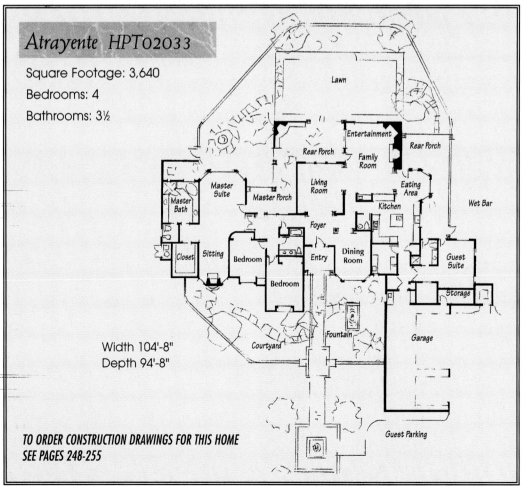

Width 104'-8"
Depth 94'-8"

TO ORDER CONSTRUCTION DRAWINGS FOR THIS HOME SEE PAGES 248-255

Satillo tile runs throughout the home, unifying the living areas and lending a Southwestern appeal to the rooms.

Opposite above: An eclectic mix of Native American, European and Mexican furnishings is well suited to the exquisite natural surroundings.

Opposite below: A private courtyard provides a contemplative fountain and a chair for stargazing.

outdoor place to unwind, engage in casual conversation or silently stargaze. Inside, state-of-the-art electronics, including a surround-sound system, are housed in custom-designed cabinetry.

The porch wraps around the rear of the home and leads to a more secluded place, dedicated to the owners wing. A wide bay window permits a fabulous view of the surrounding scenery from the owners bedroom. This rambling suite includes a spacious sitting area with a hand-carved fireplace and extravagant bath. A freestanding iron vanity and mirror with surface-mounted sink and copper faucet highlight this lavish retreat, and stone replaces tile in order to create a better connection to the environment.

DESIGNER: © Michael G. Almli Construction
Company, Inc., Tucson, Arizona
BUILDER: Michael G. Almli Construction
Company, Inc.
INTERIOR DESIGN: Robinson & Shades Interiors
PHOTOGRAPHS: © Visual Solutions Co.

ALLENDE

DESIGN BY HOME PLANNERS

STREET OF DREAMS
Allende

Next to Nature

Southwest living is all about being close to nature, and from each room of this classic desert home, one can view the wonders of the region.

This Southwestern-style home is comfortable under the blazing desert sun but it would be the talk of the town in any modern city. In an Arcadian suburb, off a country road or right in the middle of the desert, this magnificent home allows breathtaking views of nature, the best indoor and outdoor amenities, and all the modern comforts of home. Tall windows expand the views from within the home, while wide doors extend the living areas.

From the angled covered porch, the entry and foyer lead to an open arrangement of the formal rooms. Guests will take advantage of the convenient coat closet then relax in the gathering room before dinner. A raised-hearth fireplace with a wood box helps to define this spacious area, providing warmth and an aura of coziness. One wall of the gathering room contains built-in bookshelves and cabinets for displaying curios purchased at an open-air marketplace or picked up from a stroll in the

The gathering room provides space for watching TV as well as for displaying artifacts and family treasures.

desert. The formal dining room leads to the entertainment terrace.

A few steps up from the gathering room, a vestibule leads to a guest suite or study and the owners suite. An angled, raised-hearth fireplace highlights the owners bedroom. A lavish private bath begins with a walk-in closet and dressing area. Warmth radiates out in all directions from cozy wood fires, contained by a raised, semi-circular hearth. Twin lavatories, a compartmented toilet, a corner step-up whirlpool tub and separate shower complete this

The kitchen features a beehive fireplace with a bench, or banco, and art niches for curios.

Opposite: Strategically placed between the gathering room and family kitchen, the dining room provides an elegant setting .

relaxing retreat. The guest room or study provides a door to a quiet area of the front covered porch. This room has ample closet space and its own full bath.

The kitchen includes a center cooktop island with a snack counter, plenty of workspace and a corner pantry. The adjoining family kitchen features a delightful kiva fireplace and a sitting area with a built-in audio/visual center. Nearby, clustered family bedrooms share a spacious bath that has linen storage. A planning desk, laundry and service entrance from the three-car garage complete the plan.

DESIGNER: © Home Planners
PHOTOGRAPHS: © Bob Greenspan

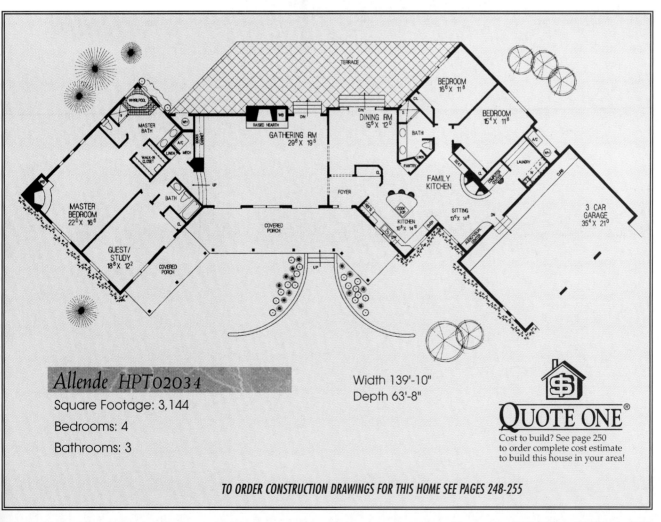

Allende HPT02034
Square Footage: 3,144
Bedrooms: 4
Bathrooms: 3

Width 139'-10"
Depth 63'-8"

QUOTE ONE®
Cost to build? See page 250 to order complete cost estimate to build this house in your area!

TO ORDER CONSTRUCTION DRAWINGS FOR THIS HOME SEE PAGES 248-255

CASABLANCA

DESIGN BY SCHAUMBERG ARCHITECTS, INC.

A True Original

With all the charm of a romantic Spanish villa, this Mediterranean beauty lends a distinctly Eastern influence to its classic curves.

Arched openings rooted in antique and classical design reveal a wealth of architectural details, inside and out, with this unique home. A Moroccan flair and dramatic interior finishes reflect an ancient culture as well as up-to-the-minute design. A stucco exterior, wrought-iron accents, spiraling columns and a magnificent tower breathe with the sense of ease and comfort of times gone by, and the mood is carried throughout the home with antique reproduced tiles and hand-applied finishes by Old World artisans. The surfaces of walls and doors are distressed for character yet ready for the future, composed of easy-maintenance natural substances such as stone, slate and granite. The color palette of the interior harmonizes with the home's beautiful surroundings, in earth tones of warm sienna, terra cotta, moss green, gold and cobalt blue.

This home, as shown in the photographs, may differ from the actual blueprints. For more detailed information, please check the floor plans carefully.

Double doors open to a two-story foyer and a floating, winding staircase. To the right, an octagonal two-story nursery features floor-to-ceiling windows and its own full bath, making it an ideal guest suite. On the opposite side of the foyer, an open study provides a fireplace, barrel-vaulted ceiling, decorative pillars and detailed molding. A few steps from a wet bar and gourmet kitchen, this area could be easily converted to a formal dining room. The well-planned kitchen is ready for all occasions, with a cooktop island counter, walk-in pantry and snack bar that seats five.

The combined formal rooms create a large, two-story space that views the pool, elevated spa and waterfall through curved twelve-foot butt-jointed glass windows. A fireplace and armoire niches provide a chic complement to wide views and natural light. Past the rear staircase, a spacious family room offers a corner fireplace, onyx wet bar, powder room and door to the covered patio. A gas grill provides an invitation to dine outdoors.

The owners suite has its own access to the rear patio, pool and spa and, of course, spectacular views. The bedroom boasts a fireplace, while the well-planned bath features a dual-sink vanity, soaking tub, separate shower and walk-in closet designed for two. This private wing is secluded behind double doors. Upstairs, a balcony hall and bridge overlook

Opposite: The owners suite opens to a lavish bath through rustic interior doors.

Right: A secondary bedroom provides a sumptuous sitting area and plenty of natural light.

Below: The foyer opens to a stately study, defined by decorative columns and a massive fireplace.

The winding central staircase overlooks an open arrangement of the formal rooms, warmed by a massive stone hearth.

The kitchen boasts rich wood accents and a soothing color palette that plays harmony with sleek chrome appliances.

Opposite: A stunning corner fireplace warms the family room—an ideal spot for cozy gatherings.

the entry and formal rooms, connect the sleeping quarters, and lead to an exterior deck. Each of the family bedrooms has a walk-in closet and private bath. The front guest suite offers a private balcony. Nearby, the media room is custom designed as a home theater with enough space for a crowd.

This original design incorporates modern materials and up-to-date amenities with the charm of Mediterranean culture. Great indoor/outdoor relationships are promoted with plenty of windows and easy access to the pool and spa. A covered breezeway connects the two-car garage with a one-car or golf-cart space, while a lovely courtyard provides a service entrance.

DESIGNER: © Schaumberg Architects, Inc., Fort Worth, Texas
BUILDER: Avalon Custom Homes
INTERIOR DESIGN: P.K. Flowers Interiors
PHOTOGRAPHS: © Visual Solutions Co.

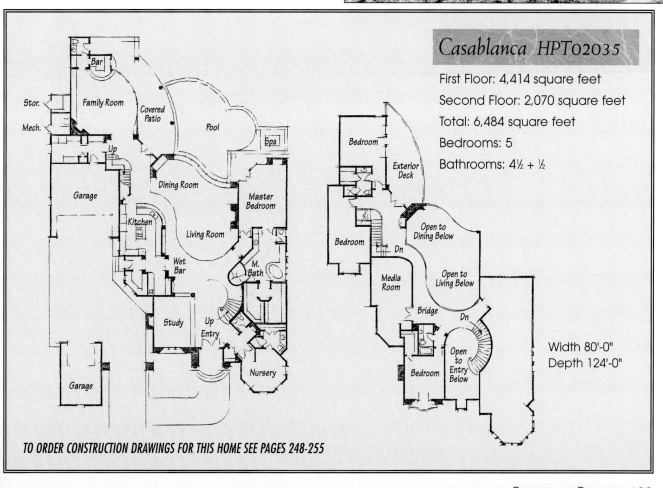

Casablanca HPT02035

First Floor: 4,414 square feet

Second Floor: 2,070 square feet

Total: 6,484 square feet

Bedrooms: 5

Bathrooms: 4½ + ½

Width 80'-0"
Depth 124'-0"

TO ORDER CONSTRUCTION DRAWINGS FOR THIS HOME SEE PAGES 248-255

CARDIFF

DESIGN BY THE SATER DESIGN COLLECTION

A Striking Presence

The graceful curves of a brick driveway announce a stunning façade with asymmetrical rooflines, gentle arches and a Mediterranean look that's refined to perfection.

The Spanish-tile roof and striking stucco exterior of this rambling single-story home introduce an interior that revisits the past in glorious style and sets a new standard for comfort and luxury. The octagonal tower features ornamental molding that lends a decorative touch to the entry, supported by stylish pillars. Double doors with sidelights brighten the foyer, which has a tray ceiling. Directly ahead, the formal living room provides views to the rear garden and fountain, and access to the covered veranda, defined by pillars. To the left of the foyer, the formal dining room features a bay window, an octagonal tray ceiling and arched alcove.

At the heart of the home, the kitchen serves the formal dining room and unifies the casual living space to the rear of the plan. This well-planned culinary retreat provides a walk-in pantry, an island counter, snack bar and plenty of counter space. Nearby, the leisure room includes two walls of windows, a tray ceiling, sliding glass door to the veranda, and a built-in entertainment center. The breakfast nook is nestled in a bay window, with access to the pool area and veranda. Outside, a summer kitchen with an island counter, pantry and grill stove make entertaining outdoors a breeze.

An arched alcove and a bay window add definition and a sense of elegance to the formal dining room.

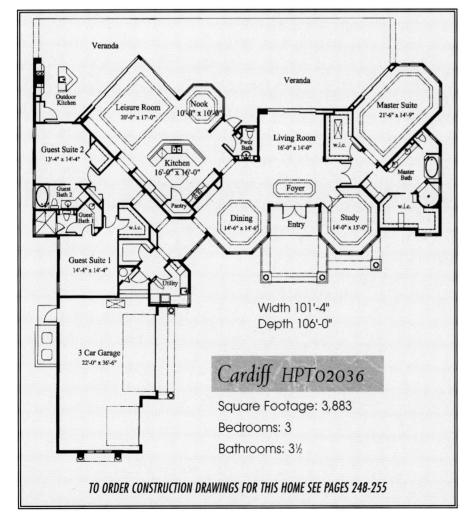

Width 101'-4"
Depth 106'-0"

Cardiff HPT02036

Square Footage: 3,883
Bedrooms: 3
Bathrooms: 3½

TO ORDER CONSTRUCTION DRAWINGS FOR THIS HOME SEE PAGES 248-255

The owners suite is secluded from the rest of the home, and double doors provide privacy. A graceful arch announces the owners bedroom. A bay window brightens the sitting area, while the pool and veranda are visible through the postless sliding glass doors. The owners bath boasts two walk-in closets and features a dual-sink vanity, garden tub and shower with seat. The secondary sleeping quarters are clustered near the informal area of the home. Each of the two guest suites to the left of the plan includes a walk-in closet and full bath—one with a garden tub and one with a shower.

Throughout the home, the creative use of arches and columns complements the extensive use of tall windows, which brighten the rooms with daylight. Great indoor/outdoor flow is accomplished with a well-planned courtyard, veranda, garden and pool area. A three-car garage provides a service entrance that leads to a laundry with a soaking sink, built-in ironing board and lots of counter space.

DESIGNER: © The Sater Design Collection
PHOTOGRAPHS: © Oscar Thompson Photography

This home, as shown in the photographs, may differ from the actual blueprints. For more detailed information, please check the floor plans carefully.

A bay window enhances the view provided by a postless sliding glass door that opens to the veranda.

Sliding glass doors open to a beautiful veranda, which is defined by a fountain and decorative pillars.

MONTERREY

DESIGN BY THE SATER DESIGN COLLECTION

Fine Lines

The richly detailed angles, curves and arches of this captivating façade provide a warm welcome to waterfront living.

This Mediterranean-style home starts with a magnificent stucco exterior, Spanish-tile roof, palm-tree landscaping and Old World details such as arches and accent niches, which frame the spectacular entry. Double French doors lead to the tiled foyer, which is brightened with natural light brought in by the fanlight above, as well as the warm glow of a centered chandelier.

To the right of the foyer, the formal dining room overlooks the front property through a wide curved wall of glass. An archway supported by decorative columns separates the dining room from the living room, which boasts a fireplace and a tray ceiling with recessed lighting. The pocket sliding glass doors open to the covered back patio, pool and spa. Six transom windows line the top of the doors, providing elegant definition to the room.

A convenient butler's pantry serves the gourmet kitchen, introduced by decorative square pillars. This well-planned room includes a corner walk-in pantry, wrapping counters, an island counter with a food-prep sink, double ovens and a six-range stove. The

Postless sliding doors extend the living area and add knock-your-socks-off views to the living room.

adjoining breakfast room provides hutch space and enjoys wide views through a curved-glass window that overlooks the pool area.

The focal point of the family room is a massive fireplace, flanked by niches and built-in cabinetry. A vaulted ceiling adds a sense of spaciousness to the room, while pocket sliding glass doors extend the living space to a wide patio with a summer kitchen. Ideal for outdoor entertaining, this area features a sink, stove and snack-bar counter. The lanai wraps around a lovely pool and spa area, creating a lavish outside retreat.

The owners suite and study occupy the opposite wing of the plan. Double French doors lead to a private vestibule with an art niche. Nearby, a thoughtfully placed powder room is convenient for guests as well as swimmers, who can access this half

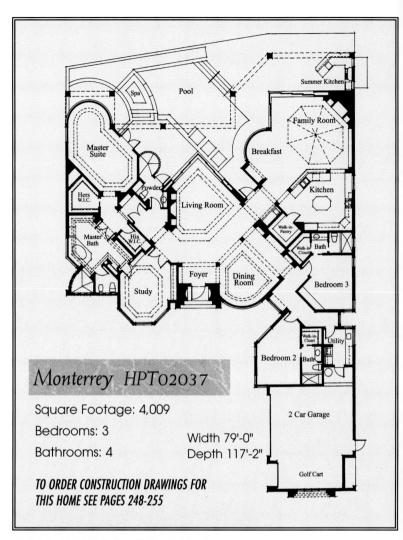

Monterrey HPT02037

Square Footage: 4,009
Bedrooms: 3
Bathrooms: 4
Width 79'-0"
Depth 117'-2"

TO ORDER CONSTRUCTION DRAWINGS FOR THIS HOME SEE PAGES 248-255

An octagonal ceiling defines the family room, which boasts a cozy fireplace and built-in bookshelves.

The owners bath surrounds a whirlpool tub with custom-built cabinetry and a row of clerestory windows.

The foyer offers interior vistas of the wide-open formal spaces and wide views of the pool and spa area.

This home, as shown in the photographs, may differ from the actual blueprints. For more detailed information, please check the floor plans carefully.

bath from the lanai. The owners bedroom opens through an archway and features a wall of glass around an ideal space that serves as a sitting area. Nearby, double doors lead out to the patio and pool. Two walk-in closets flank the entrance to the owners bath. A soaking tub features views of a side garden, while the step-up shower boasts glazed glass-block windows.

French doors open from the foyer to the quiet study, which is highlighted by a tray ceiling and defined by built-in bookshelves and richly detailed cabinetry. This room is brightened by a bay window, which overlooks the front property. The owners bath provides a separate door to the study, which is a great place for the fortunate homeowner to find repose or enjoy a good read. Each of two secondary bedrooms has a walk-in closet and full bath with shower. A gallery hall connects the guest or family sleeping quarters with a utility area.

DESIGNER: © The Sater Design Collection
PHOTOGRAPHS: © Laurence Taylor

Space Age Beauty

Graceful rooflines and a unique porte cochere complement a vaulted entry that suggests the grand, luxurious feel that fills this spectacular 21st-Century design.

Vaulted gables that point toward heaven enhance an eye-catching exterior with plenty of curb appeal. Inside, the ease and comfort of a thoroughly modern home projects a uniquely chic attitude—both formal and practical. Quiet outdoor spaces add a natural touch, beginning with the covered walkway, private garden and fountain that surround the entry. A wraparound veranda to the rear of the plan sports an outdoor kitchen, complete with a grill and cooktop.

Casual and formal rooms use the outdoor areas to extend the home's living space and take full advantage of the views provided through walls of glass. To the left of the foyer, the formal dining room features a built-in server and double French doors that lead to a front

THE MONTESINO
DESIGN BY ERIC S. BROWN'S
PALLADIAN DESIGN COLLECTION

This home, as shown in the photographs, may differ from the actual blueprints. For more detailed information, please check the floor plans carefully.

garden and fountain—an ideal place for dinner guests to linger. The heart of the home is a grand, two-story parlor with a coffered ceiling. A bay window and two sets of French doors leading to the veranda contribute to an aura of spaciousness, while a fireplace and built-ins make it cozy.

A first-floor guest suite has a private porch and a bath that serves as a pool cabana. The owners suite features a built-in niche, glass doors to the veranda and a stunning sitting retreat that's brightened by a bay window. Separate vanities and walk-in closets

STREET OF DREAMS
The Montesino

accommodate two homeowners. A lavish bath with a garden tub, separate shower and sauna add to the luxury of this suite. An alcove leads to a private study with a tray ceiling and built-ins.

A circular, floating stairway and an adjacent elevator both lead upstairs to the secondary sleeping quarters. A media loft

Opposite: The dazzling pool, spa and patio create a relaxing outdoor retreat.

A magnificent fireplace, mantel and mirror highlight the parlor, which opens to the veranda.

French doors open formal dining room a luxuriant garden and fountain.

with hardwood floors overlooks the parlor and dining room. Double doors open to an extensive upper deck that offers views of the veranda, pool and spa. Each of the two guest suites on the second floor includes a walk-in closet, full bath and private access to the deck. Above the garage, a bonus room with two dormer windows, a corner walk-in closet, built-ins and a full bath offers the possibility of a fourth bedroom, home office, mother-in-law suite or recreation space.

DESIGNER: © Eric S. Brown's *Palladian Design Collection*
PHOTOGRAPHS: © Laurence Taylor Architectural Photography

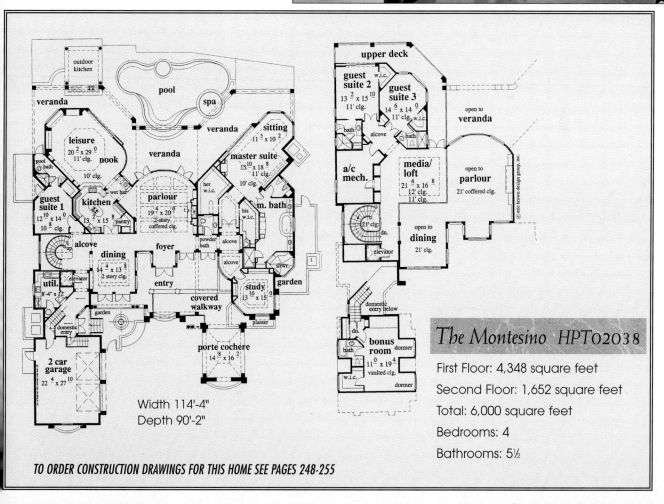

The Montesino HPT02038

First Floor: 4,348 square feet

Second Floor: 1,652 square feet

Total: 6,000 square feet

Bedrooms: 4

Bathrooms: 5½

Width 114'-4"
Depth 90'-2"

TO ORDER CONSTRUCTION DRAWINGS FOR THIS HOME SEE PAGES 248-255

NEWPORT

DESIGN BY THE SATER DESIGN COLLECTION

On the Waterfront

Savory comfort hugs a sun-kissed coastal classic that boasts modern open space and dreamy views.

A romantic air flirts with the clean simple lines of this seaside home, where ocean breezes travel freely from front to back. Open and sophisticated, its broad interior is made cozy by a refined decor that's also sweetly unpretentious and downright comfortable. An enchanting mix of exotic textiles and delicate but durable European furnishings exalts a muted palette well suited for a coastal retreat. Soaring ceilings add a sense of spaciousness, while a sprawling lanai blurs the line between

Retreating glass doors allow a put-your-feet-up atmosphere in the heart of the home.

STREET OF DREAMS
Newport

outdoors and in—a perfect arrangement for both traditional events as well as intimate gatherings.

The entry's fanlight brightens the two-story foyer, which enjoys engaging views through the living area's two full walls of windows. French doors open to a quiet study with built-in bookshelves and a tall window, which looks out to the front property. A planter outside the window encourages the growth of foliage to frame the view. This room features an elegant tray ceiling and provides space for reading, relaxing and quiet conversation with guests.

A sunlit leisure room with its own fireplace allows sights

Silk and tapestry set off a chic blend of furnishings in the living room, which opens to the lanai.

Opposite: A stunning tray ceiling crowns the elegant formal dining room, which enjoys front-facing views.

This gormet kitchen has a food-prep island counter. The plan provides a center cooktop as well as an angled counter with a double sink.

of nature and helps bring in a sense of the out-doors. The living and dining rooms are open to one another, defined by coffered ceilings. The well-appointed kitchen overlooks an island counter with a double sink and shares a view of the lanai with the breakfast nook. An outdoor kitchen allows easy meals and invites a "lose the shoes" attitude beyond the leisure room.

An angled wing harbors a rambling owners suite with a bay window and a wall of glass that opens through sliding doors to the lanai. A private vestibule leads from the owners bedroom to a dressing area with a three-way mirror and a walk-in closet designed for two.

DESIGNER: © The Sater Design Collection
PHOTOGRAPHS: © Laurence Taylor
Architectural Photography

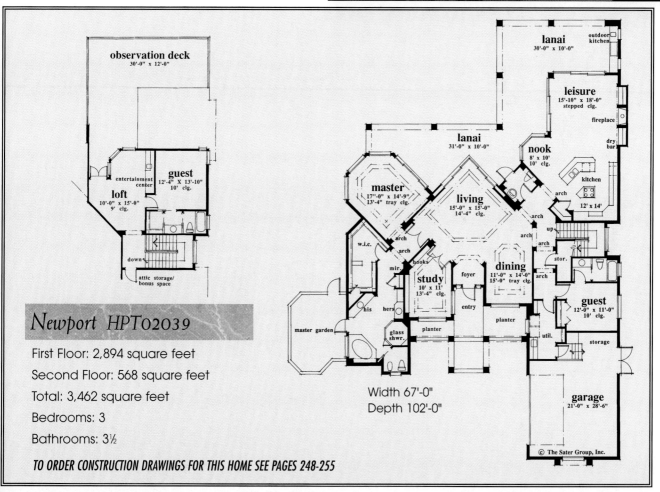

Newport HPT02039

First Floor: 2,894 square feet

Second Floor: 568 square feet

Total: 3,462 square feet

Bedrooms: 3

Bathrooms: 3½

Width 67'-0"
Depth 102'-0"

TO ORDER CONSTRUCTION DRAWINGS FOR THIS HOME SEE PAGES 248-255

WINDSOR BAY

Light Catcher

A magnificent turret announces this stately design, dressed with wide-open views, walls of glass and supremely comfortable amenities.

A courtyard entry defines the façade of this sprawling Mediterranean-style home. The plan's focus is the interior courtyard, with a pool, spa, waterfall, koi pond, bridges and a series of sun decks and patios. An outdoor kitchen is ideal for dining alfresco. Two identical guest suites flank the double-door courtyard entry. These suites feature corner windows overlooking the courtyard, and each has a kitchenette and a bath with a dual-sink vanity, soaking tub and separate shower. Placed away from the main house, these suites provide both privacy and comfort.

The main house has two entries, one near the owners suite and another that leads to the leisure room and kitchen. The informal living space includes a bay window

A few steps up from the owners suite, a sumptuous sitting retreat is warmed by a fireplace.

6559

STREET OF DREAMS
Windsor Bay

and sliding glass doors to an outdoor deck. A staircase just off the leisure room leads to the upstairs bonus room, attic space and second-story deck, perfect for viewing the backyard. Two islands enhance the kitchen's function. Each includes a sink and extensive counter space, while a four-stool snack bar provides a casual eating area. Pass through the gallery to the dining room, highlighted by a buffet server and two walls of windows that overlook the pool and bridge. A pantry and spacious laundry room, with a soaking sink, built-in ironing board and ample counter and cabinet space, are nearby. The three-car garage is located close to the kitchen and opens to the side of the house.

A corner bar, tray ceiling with recessed lighting and two sliding glass doors highlight the gathering room. An alcove entry connects the gathering room to the owners suite. The owners bedroom boasts built-in units, a tray ceiling with detailed molding, and corner windows with views of the backyard and private garden. An octagonal-shaped study

This home, as shown in the photographs, may differ from the actual blueprints. For more detailed information, please check the floor plans carefully.

The owners bath features a chic whirlpool tub and surround, a separate shower and two walk-in closets.

Opposite: A splendid waterfall enhances one of three enchanting pools, surrounded by lush greenery, a sun deck and two stately gazebos.

Each of two food-prep islands in the kitchen provides a sink and plenty of counter space.

adjoins the bedroom and includes built-in bookshelves, a bay window overlooking the pool and courtyard, and a separate entrance from the veranda. Double doors invite owners to the bath, which features two walk-in closets lit by small windows, a dual-sink vanity, a walk-in shower and a soaking tub with sliding glass doors that open to the private garden. From the owners bedroom, four steps lead to a retreat room with a fireplace, corner built-ins, and opposing decks. Completing the plan is the private garden, which includes a pool, bridge and sun deck.

DESIGNER: © The Sater Design Collection
PHOTOGRAPHS: © Oscar Thompson Photography

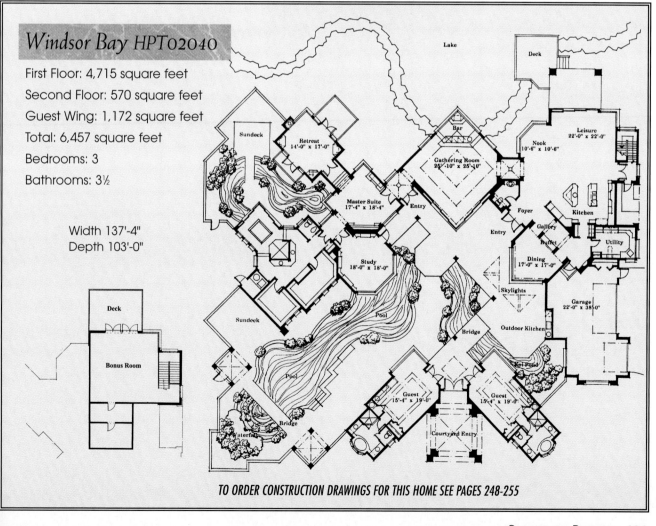

Windsor Bay HPT02040

First Floor: 4,715 square feet
Second Floor: 570 square feet
Guest Wing: 1,172 square feet
Total: 6,457 square feet
Bedrooms: 3
Bathrooms: 3½

Width 137'-4"
Depth 103'-0"

Deck
Bonus Room

Lake
Deck
Sundeck
Retreat 14'-0" x 17'-0"
Bar
Gathering Room 25'-10" x 25'-10"
Leisure 22'-0" x 22'-0"
Nook 10'-6" x 10'-6"
Master Suite 17'-4" x 18'-4"
Entry
Foyer
Kitchen
Entry
Gallery
Study 18'-0" x 18'-0"
Buffet
Utility
Dining 17'-0" x 17'-0"
Skylights
Garage 22'-0" x 38'-0"
Sundeck
Pool
Bridge
Outdoor Kitchen
Koi Pond
Pool
Guest 15'-4" x 19'-0"
Guest 15'-4" x 19'-0"
Bridge
Waterfall
Courtyard Entry

TO ORDER CONSTRUCTION DRAWINGS FOR THIS HOME SEE PAGES 248-255

THE PROVENCE

DESIGN BY ERIC S. BROWN'S *PALLADIAN DESIGN COLLECTION*

STREET OF DREAMS
The Provence

An arch-top window allows even nighttime views
to enhance the parlor.

Domestic Bliss

A sweet sense of casual elegance prevails in this sophisticated design, creating an atmosphere that's easy to call home.

Stucco and shingles adorn the beautiful façade of this award-winning plan. A covered port cochere shelters guests from the elements and provides a proper introduction to a home that it would be easy to fall in love with. A magnificent entry leads to a spacious, well-lit foyer, where a broad interior vista takes in the grand parlor and extends to the sweeping rear veranda, pool and spa.

A fifteen-foot-high ceiling in the formal parlor creates a sense of grandeur, enhanced by open views. An ornately carved stone fireplace warms this room and makes it a cozy place to gather. An alcove with a barrel-vaulted ceiling connects the formal area with a spacious leisure room. The covered veranda extends the

The leisure room over-
looks the lake and rear
patio—a calming
retreat that includes
a fountain.

THE PROVENCE

casual living space: slide back the glass doors and the room will
effectively double in size.

A well-equipped kitchen has a center food-prep island counter,
an arched niche with recessed lighting above the cooktop, and
wrapping counter space. A butler's pantry connects the kitchen
with the formal dining room, where a vaulted ceiling and double
doors to a wide balcony increase the aura of spaciousness. A
gallery hall leads to a sizable walk-in pantry and utility area. Twin
sets of French doors open from the hall to a stunning front patio
and courtyard.

To the right of the plan, an alcove announces two sets of double doors that open to the owners suite and private parlor, which easily converts to a study. This secluded room features a barrel-vaulted ceiling and a door to the front balcony. Across the alcove, a wide hall leads to His and Hers walk-in closets. The owners bedroom features a sliding glass wall that opens to a private area of the veranda. Three windows offer splendid outdoor views and brighten a sitting area—a cozy retreat for a quiet read. The owners bath includes a walk-in shower, separate vanities and a glorious whirlpool tub with a garden view.

To the left of the plan, two lavish guest suites share an alcove that opens from the leisure room and leads outdoors to a lovely garden patio. The rear guest suite features a door to a private patio, pool and spa area, veranda and outdoor kitchen. The suite offers a walk-in closet and a full bath, which also serves as a pool bath. The front guest suite provides a walk-in shower, compartmented toilet, built-in bookshelves and a wide window that offers views to the garden patio.

Culinary artists will appreciate the food-prep island and wrapping counters of the gourmet kitchen.

The expansive rear veranda is the real jewel of this home and may be the most popular spot in the plan. An outdoor kitchen provides all of the necessary tools for whipping up a great afternoon meal. Planters wrap around the inviting pool and therapeutic spa, adding a superb touch of style and color to the outdoor area.

DESIGNER: © Eric S. Brown's *Palladian Design Collection*
BUILDER: Harwick Homes
PHOTOGRAPHS: © Dan Forer
© Oscar Thompson Photography (Exterior)

A casual dining nook shares a warm ambience with the leisure room.

Opposite: Separate vanities and a whirlpool tub create a sumptuous owners bath.

Walls of windows brighten the owners suite, which includes a spacious sitting area.

The Provence HPT02041

First Floor: 4,762 square feet

Second Floor: 775 square feet

Total: 5,537 square feet

Bedrooms: 4

Bathrooms: 4½

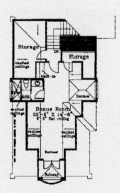

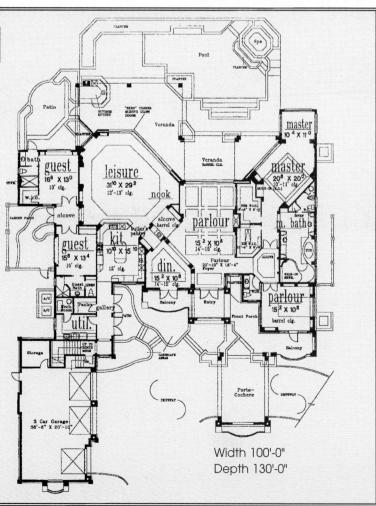

Width 100'-0"
Depth 130'-0"

*TO ORDER CONSTRUCTION DRAWINGS FOR THIS
HOME SEE PAGES 248-255*

THE MARSALLA

DESIGN BY ERIC S. BROWN'S *PALLADIAN DESIGN COLLECTION*

Classic Elegance

A traditional yet dazzling mix of stucco detailing and dramatic rooflines give this Sun Country gem a clean, elegant feel.

This award-winning design is arranged in a flowing, open layout that uses richly detailed architectural elements, such as arches, columns and alcoves, to define the living and dining spaces. A covered glass double-door entry leads through the foyer to the central formal parlor which features a dramatic coffered ceilng, a warming fireplace, built-in bookshelves, a stunning planter and sliding glass doors to the rear

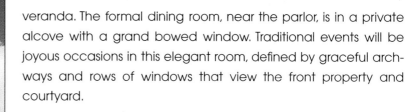

veranda. The formal dining room, near the parlor, is in a private alcove with a grand bowed window. Traditional events will be joyous occasions in this elegant room, defined by graceful archways and rows of windows that view the front property and courtyard.

Comfortable living is guaranteed in the open leisure room, surrounded by walls of glass. A built-in entertainment center is framed by wide views of the stunning pool area. Sliding corner doors open this space to a rambling veranda that includes an

The parlor features corner sliding doors to the rear veranda and planter, a warming fireplace and stunning ceiling detail.

outdoor cooking center and eating bar. An open skylight tops a secluded niche of the veranda, guarded by a privacy wall, creating an ideal place to enjoy meals outside.

The leisure room opens to a morning nook and eating bar, both served by the kitchen. A sizable island counter complements the extensive wrapping counters. A bay window overlooks the veranda and brings in plenty of daylight.

A gallery hall leads through a series of stunning archways, past the kitchen to a guest suite. This spacious bedroom boasts a walk-in closet, full bath with a garden tub, and sliding glass-door access to the veranda. Nearby, a thoughtfully placed powder room maintains privacy for the guestroom. Guest Suite 2 is detached from the main house, connected only by

Wide views surround the formal dining room, enhanced by a tray ceiling.

Luxuriant vistas frame the entertainment center in the leisure room—a breezy space near an outdoor kitchen.

the veranda. This wonderful retreat features a wet bar, a triple window, plenty of wardrobe space and a lavish bath with an oversized shower. This full bath is also convenient to the pool area.

A gallery hall, with French doors and archways announcing a private garden, library, dressing area and walk-in closet, connects the rooms of the owners wing. A lavish private bath features separate vanities, a spacious bedroom and a secluded retreat with doors to the veranda. A triple window brightens this area, while a row of windows in the bath offers views to an enchanting garden. Richly hued stone flooring with intricate detailing matches the countertops in this spacious chamber.

Lush gardens frame the library, which provides a lovely bowed window and vaulted ceiling. Secluded by the central gallery hall, this room could easily convert to a home office, exercise room or quiet study. At the other end of the hall, a service wing features a utility room, linen storage and a door to the three-car garage.

The Marsalla HPT02042

Square Footage: 4,575
Bedrooms: 3
Bathrooms: 3½

TO ORDER CONSTRUCTION DRAWINGS FOR THIS HOME SEE PAGES 248-255

DESIGNER: © Eric S. Brown's
*Palladian Design
Collection*
PHOTOGRAPHS: © Oscar Thompson
Photography

Corner doors open the parlor to the rear veranda, extending the living space and creating views.

LA CORUNA

DESIGN BY THE SATER DESIGN COLLECTION

House and Garden

One-of-a-kind details give this slightly European exterior a unique look that harmonizes sweetly with a lush garden, courtyard and patio.

The scored stucco columns, curved walls of glass, grille window details and the wooden trellis add plenty of excitement to this romantic design but the real beauty lies in its relationship to the outdoors. The entry courtyard is designed to grab a slice of nature, create an enticingly simple mood and soothe the soul. A koi pond enhances the meditative spirit of the front grounds.

The detailed front exterior boasts a koi pond.

STREET OF DREAMS
La Coruna

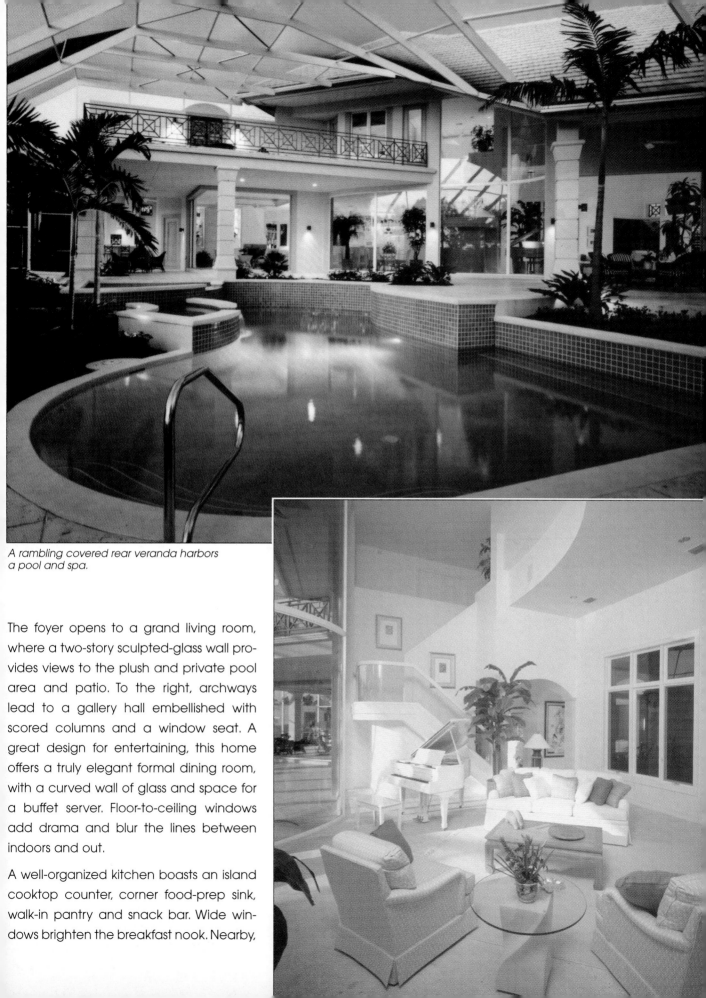

A rambling covered rear veranda harbors a pool and spa.

The foyer opens to a grand living room, where a two-story sculpted-glass wall provides views to the plush and private pool area and patio. To the right, archways lead to a gallery hall embellished with scored columns and a window seat. A great design for entertaining, this home offers a truly elegant formal dining room, with a curved wall of glass and space for a buffet server. Floor-to-ceiling windows add drama and blur the lines between indoors and out.

A well-organized kitchen boasts an island cooktop counter, corner food-prep sink, walk-in pantry and snack bar. Wide windows brighten the breakfast nook. Nearby,

the leisure room provides plenty of space to spread out and relax. The corner pocket sliding glass doors fully disappear into the walls, making the covered veranda a stunning extension of the room. Eye-catching details include a vaulted ceiling, fireplace and wet bar. An outdoor kitchen and cabana bath complete this informal entertainment area.

The unique angled layout of this plan continues in the owners wing. In the private foyer, art niches flank a full-length dressing mirror. An archway leads to the owners bedroom, where glass pocket double doors open to the covered veranda and a bay window surrounds a sitting area. The owners bath features two walk-in closets, a knee-space vanity and a step-up shower. The soaking tub looks out through a mitered-glass window to a private garden and privacy wall.

This home, as shown in the photographs, may differ from the actual blueprints. For more detailed information, please check the floor plans carefully.

Gentle arches announce the spacious living room— a great place to entertain formally or just throw a comfortable bash.

Opposite: Sleek cabinets and countertops set off a subtle décor in the kitchen.

Elegance prevails in the formal dining room, where a curved wall of glass, fills the space with natural light.

A first-floor guestroom provides a walk-in closet, full bath and French-door access to a lovely side garden. A separate studio, or additional guest suite, has its own bath—this space would easily convert to a home office, recreation room or atelier. Upstairs, the loft adds space for entertaining. The second-floor guest suite has a vaulted ceiling, sitting area, walk-in closet and observation deck.

DESIGNER: © The Sater Design Collection

PHOTOGRAPHS: © Oscar Thompson Photography

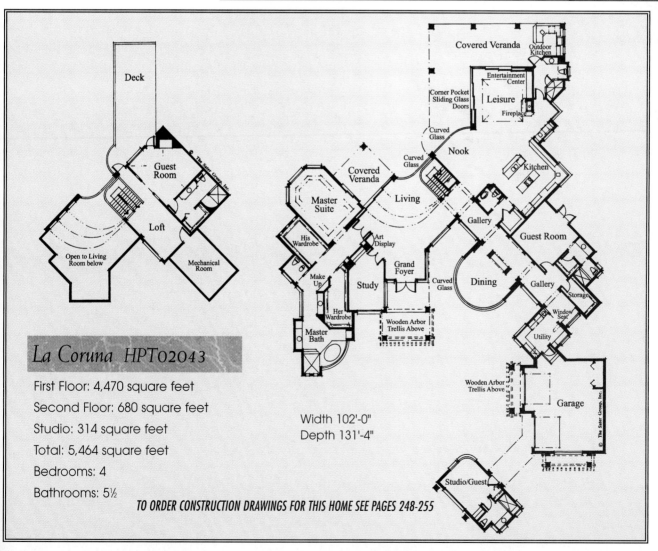

La Coruna HPT02043

First Floor: 4,470 square feet

Second Floor: 680 square feet

Studio: 314 square feet

Total: 5,464 square feet

Bedrooms: 4

Bathrooms: 5½

Width 102'-0"
Depth 131'-4"

TO ORDER CONSTRUCTION DRAWINGS FOR THIS HOME SEE PAGES 248-255

space beside the entry that provides protection and lends a stately presence to the front of the home. A well-planned interior reveals that wide-open space, high ceilings and walls of windows can be supremely grand yet not intimidating. Sculpture is found throughout the home in arched room entrances, beautiful mold-

THE AUGUSTA

DESIGN BY ERIC S. BROWN'S
PALLADIAN DESIGN COLLECTION

Grand Simplicity

Lavish amenities accomplish more than grand aesthetics—they set a tone that unites this award-winning home with its outdoor setting.

Straightforward lines, a wraparound veranda, high-pitched rooflines and a host of atriums blur the separation between the living areas of this stunning stucco home and the natural world that surrounds it. A covered porte cochere creates a drive-through

ings, indoor columns, wall reliefs and fireplace surrounds. With livable spaces, flexible rooms, richly sculpted detail and an estate-style presence, this design creates a custom look that calls up the past but is ready for the future.

Long views through the parlor look toward the pool, courtyard and veranda, while the dining room faces the front garden. A beautiful bowed window and tray ceiling help to define this formal room, which offers a view of a lovely side atrium. The leisure room provides a curved window wall that overlooks a luxuriant planter and offers French-door

Opposite: The formal living room includes gorgeous natural views and arches.

STREET OF DREAMS
The Augusta

access to the rear veranda. A window seat in the central gallery hall looks past an alcove to a beautiful side-yard atrium.

The kitchen boasts a planning desk, walk-in pantry, center cooktop island with prep sink, and an eat-in table in the morning nook. Granite surfaces and stone columns add drama and elegance to the heart of this home. A double-sink counter overlooks the leisure room, which has a vaulted ceiling. Built-in

cabinetry, a fireplace and a cozy alcove with breathtaking views of the veranda make this casual space entirely livable.

The owners suite is a truly opulent retreat. Double doors lead to a secluded study with built-in shelves and a tray ceiling. Built-in desk space and a sizable storage closet make the room perfect for a home office or library. A single door leads to the owners exercise room, also accessed from the center hall and from the

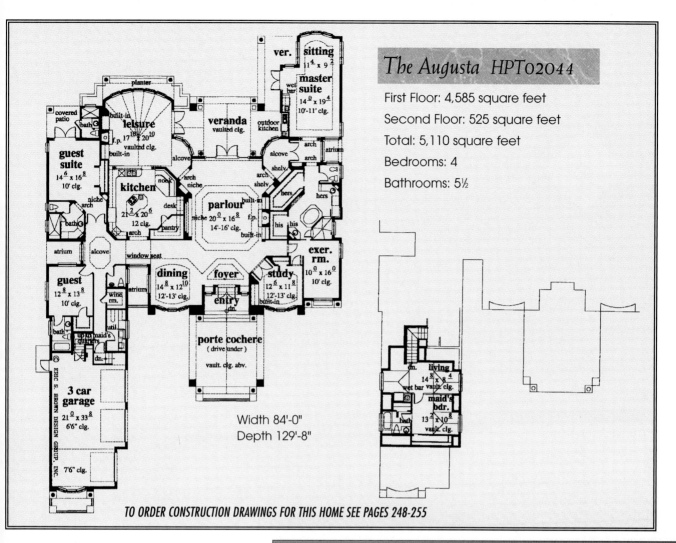

TO ORDER CONSTRUCTION DRAWINGS FOR THIS HOME SEE PAGES 248-255

The Augusta HPT02044

First Floor: 4,585 square feet

Second Floor: 525 square feet

Total: 5,110 square feet

Bedrooms: 4

Bathrooms: 5½

Width 84'-0"
Depth 129'-8"

bath through a sliding pocket door. This mirrored room could also be used as a nursery or hobby room. The owners bedroom provides a wet bar, sitting area, tray ceiling, bay window and doors to the veranda and outdoor kitchen. Arches and glass walls surround a private atrium that helps to separate the owners bedroom and bath. His and Hers vanities, two walk-in closets, an island soaking tub and an etched-glass shower finish this idyllic retreat.

DESIGNER: © Eric S. Brown's *Palladian Design Collection*

PHOTOGRAPHS: © Oscar Thompson Photography

This home, as shown in the photographs, may differ from the actual blueprints. For more detailed information, please check the floor plans carefully.

THE HAMPTON

DESIGN BY FRANK SALAMONE, NEWLINE DESIGN

Cool Digs

With over 4,000 square feet of living space, this way-past-cool design allows universal mobility, an ease of living and plenty of space to work and entertain.

Asymmetrical gables, tall, narrow windows and stately brick pillars lend a futuristic appearance and loads of curb appeal to this universal design. Doorways and hallways are wide, living spaces are open and all of the areas of the home are easily reached, maneuverable and light-filled. This modern, efficient design is remarkably well

This home, as shown in the photographs, may differ from the actual blueprints. For more detailed information, please check the floor plans carefully.

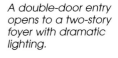

A double-door entry opens to a two-story foyer with dramatic lighting.

equipped with high style and practical rooms packed with up-to-the-minute amenities. The creative floor plan and impressive façade create a home that's perfect for entertaining as well as raising a family.

The central foyer features dramatic lighting and a tile floor that's easily reached from a stepless columned front porch. Double doors are framed with sidelights and transoms that reflect the modern mood of the entire home. The foyer leads to a spacious great room, where skylights and floor-to-ceiling windows bathe the area with daylight—or sometimes moonlight. A circular aquarium echoes the architectural theme of the casual living space and morning nook, with lots of curves and smooth angles.

the kitchen from the second-floor hallway, adding to the open feeling. The formal dining room opens to both the kitchen and the great room—a perfect arrangement for entertaining, whether the occasion is a planned event or an informal gathering. A vaulted ceiling adds a sense of spaciousness to the living area, while the curved aquarium and a see-through fireplace make it cozy.

A rambling owners suite is designed for luxury. Crowned with a tray ceiling, the open

The skylit great room features a half-round aquarium, a warm hearth, floor-to-ceiling windows, a continuation of the foyer's tiled floor and many maneuverable spaces.

The work areas in the kitchen are arranged in a circular pattern for convenience, enclosing an island counter with dual heights. The sink, range and counters are placed at seated heights for ease of use. Wide aisles, under-counter drawers and adjustable work areas make this room a gourmet's delight. A glass wall peers into

Opposite: Wonderfully open areas define the owners bedroom, which is cheered by a fireplace that's shared by the great room.

The kitchen is a cook's dream, with ulta-modern appliances and plenty of counter and work space.

bedroom is warmed by the through-fireplace shared with the great room. Clerestory windows infuse the suite with soft, ambient light. His and Hers dressing areas and walk-in closets with adjustable storage systems enhance this wonderful retreat.

To the right of the plan, a quiet study features a wall of built-in shelves and lovely twin windows. Nearby, a hall defined by decorative columns and an art niche leads to a convenient powder room and walk-in coat closet.

DESIGNER: © Frank Salamone, Newline Design
BUILDER: G. L. Witt
PHOTOGRAPHS: © Bob Greenspan

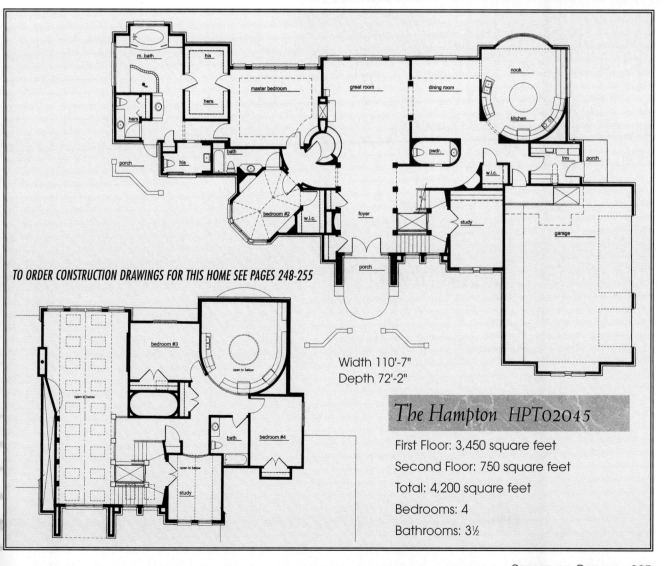

TO ORDER CONSTRUCTION DRAWINGS FOR THIS HOME SEE PAGES 248-255

Width 110'-7"
Depth 72'-2"

The Hampton HPT02045

First Floor: 3,450 square feet

Second Floor: 750 square feet

Total: 4,200 square feet

Bedrooms: 4

Bathrooms: 3½

THE ARTISAN

DESIGN BY EDWARDS COMPANY

Modern Rustic

Classic lines and simple, high-pitched roofs make a straightforward, oh-so-chic statement about living next to nature in a home that's thoroughly up-to-date.

This charming two-story cottage-style home represents the rich tradition and architecture of Yolo County, California, with prominent gables, intricate exterior wood details and an inviting front sitting porch. Designed for a 21st-Century lifestyle, the custom home overlooks Lake Alhambra and features an

expansive open-beam ceiling in the casual living space. Most of the first floor features beautiful rich maple hardwood flooring, which harmonizes with rustic African-slate tile and hearty soft-hued carpeting. Hand-painted murals and faux effects such as *trompe l'oeil* give this home a sweet-and-stunning personality. Extra-high ceilings, coffered in a variety of styles, create a sense of spaciousness throughout the home.

A New England copper-roofed cupola features a verde "antique bike" weathervane that cues the visitor on what's to come inside: a delightful collection of antique bicycles as well as treasures gathered from the local emporiums. Prominent gables, nat-

A beautifully detailed formal dining room opens to an area of the living room that's perfect for a piano.

STREET OF DREAMS
The Artisan

ural stone veneer and Doric-style columns announce a unique interior that starts with an angled foyer. Thoughtfully designed, traditional in style and elegantly classic, the home is beautifully detailed, with amenities that cater to an ease of living and satisfy the technological demands of the future. The wide-open arrangement of the formal rooms allows interior vistas that extend to an idyllic courtyard and garden. The living room includes a space perfectly suited for a piano. Handmade light fixtures comple-ment an impressive collection of paintings by local artists in this formal area—an ideal space for entertaining.

A walk-in pantry and servery separates the formal dining room from the kitchen. Some of the remarkable amenities of this culinary paradise include custom-designed cabinetry, handcrafted light fixtures over the central cooktop island, stainless-steel ovens, a paneled dishwasher and a marble counter and glass rack in the butler's pantry. The mix of beauty and quality continues in the morning nook, which nestles in a dazzling bay window. Antique hand-loomed rugs cover the hardwood floors.

The family room boasts a high-beam ceiling and an inviting marble-faced wood-burning fireplace with a handcrafted mantel. Glass-fronted custom cabinets complement window transoms and lovely French doors that lead to a lakeside garden. A food-prep counter overlooks the family room from the kitchen, allowing the cook to participate in conversations.

The owners suite and sitting area lead to a patio that overlooks the gardens. The bath features a tile tub surround, custom vanity cabinets in alder, walk-in

Above: An open-beam cathedral ceiling complements recessed lighting, a wood-burning fireplace and maple hardwood floors in the family room.

Opposite: An impressive bay window and gas fireplace enhance the owners bedroom, which opens to a study or guest suite.

Custom cabinetry, handcrafted light fixtures and a six-burner cooktop stove highlight the gourmet kitchen.

closets and a glass-block double shower. A marble-faced gas fireplace warms both the bedroom and tub area of the bath. A wrapping vanity provides separate lavatories. Tucked away to the rear of the plan, a study with its own bath could easily serve as a guest suite, home office or private den for the homeowners.

DESIGNER: © Edwards Company, Loomis, California
BUILDER: Monley-Cronin Construction
INTERIOR DESIGN: Design House Furniture Galleries
PHOTOGRAPHS: © Visual Solutions Co.

This home, as shown in the photographs, may differ from the actual blueprints. For more detailed information, please check the floor plans carefully.

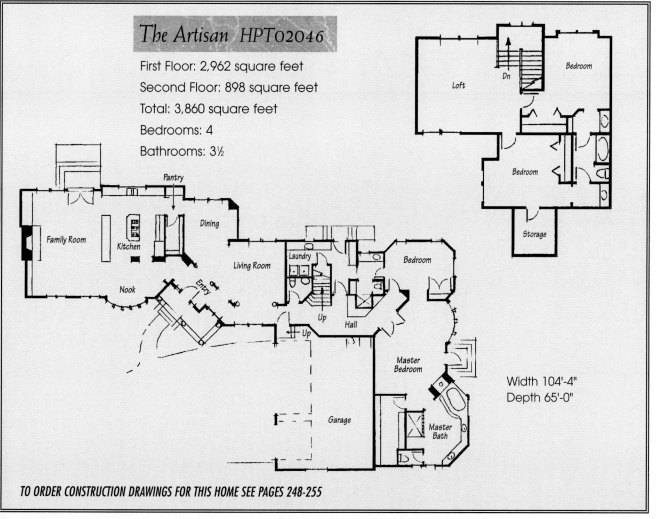

The Artisan HPT02046

First Floor: 2,962 square feet

Second Floor: 898 square feet

Total: 3,860 square feet

Bedrooms: 4

Bathrooms: 3½

Width 104'-4"
Depth 65'-0"

TO ORDER CONSTRUCTION DRAWINGS FOR THIS HOME SEE PAGES 248-255

STREET OF DREAMS
Southwind

SOUTHWIND

DESIGN BY STEPHEN FULLER, AMERICAN HOME GALLERY

Royal Retreat

A charming low-country home with amenities that do more than just dazzle invites the ease and comfort of true luxury.

The elegant, two-story foyer of this traditional design features a dramatic oak staircase with careful details that help establish a theme of relaxed living and high style. The heart of the first floor is the spacious great room, which features a built-in entertainment center and wet bar. A massive fireplace with an extended hearth warms this spacious area, which boasts panoramic views of the rear property. Across the gallery hall, an elegant dining room is richly furnished with a hand-decorated sisal rug and custom stencil motif on the walls. To the right of the foyer, a formal living room or parlor has its own fireplace. Nearby, a generous guestroom provides private access to a full bath.

The open-concept kitchen offers state-of-the-art appliances, oak cabinets and recessed lighting. Wrapping counters and a double sink enjoy plenty of light and wide views from a window bay surrounding a morning nook. The center cooktop island counter allows the chef to participate in morning conversations while whipping up

Inset: A highly detailed balustrade defines the foyer stairs and sets off a stunning red oak hardwood floor.

Classic furnishings set a relaxed theme in the living room.

Opposite: An inviting portico leads to the walkout basement, which provides space for an exercise room.

The great room features a beam ceiling, fireplace, and built-in entertainment center.

pancakes or crepes suzette. A rear staircase provides the second-floor bedrooms with easy access to the breakfast area.

Upstairs, a five-star owners suite begins with a spacious bedroom and tray ceiling. A bay window surrounds a stunning sitting area, allowing wide views of the rear gardens. In the private bath, a whirlpool tub is flanked by separate vanities with framed bath mirrors. Across the gallery hall, one of the secondary bedrooms has its own full bath and plenty of wardrobe space—a perfect arrangement for a live-in relative or guest. On the

other side of the balcony hall, two family bedrooms share a full bath that provides separate lavatories.

The unfinished walkout basement provides the possibility of a second guest suite and a media room. Glass doors allow great views of the golf course and lead to an outdoor area. A few steps up, the deck features a gas grill and opens conveniently from the breakfast nook and kitchen.

DESIGNER: © Stephen Fuller,
American Home Gallery
BUILDER: Premier Design Concepts, Inc.
INTERIOR DESIGN: Beverly Hall Furniture Galleries
PHOTOGRAPHS: © Visual Solutions Co.,
Courtesy of Stephen Fuller,
American Home Gallery

This home, as shown in the photographs, may differ from the actual blueprints. For more detailed information, please check the floor plans carefully.

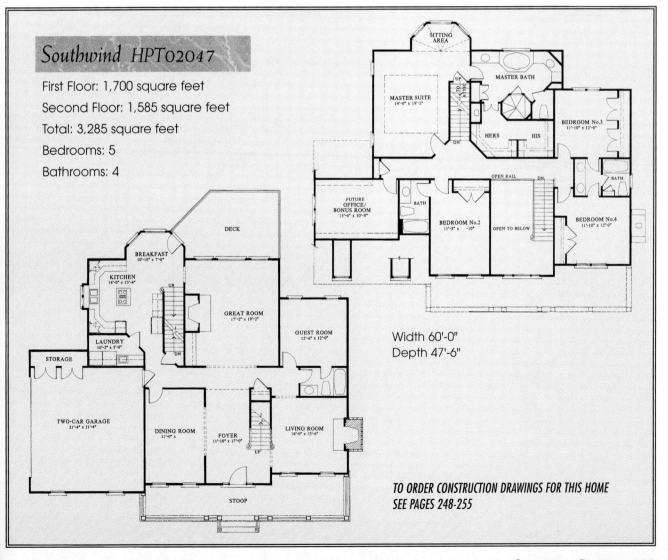

Southwind HPT02047

First Floor: 1,700 square feet

Second Floor: 1,585 square feet

Total: 3,285 square feet

Bedrooms: 5

Bathrooms: 4

SITTING AREA

MASTER SUITE
14'-0" x 19'-2"

MASTER BATH

UP

HERS   HIS

BEDROOM No.3
11'-10" x 12'-0"

DN

FUTURE OFFICE/ BONUS ROOM
15'-6" x 10'-8"

BATH

OPEN RAIL

DN

BATH

BEDROOM No.2
11'-8" x -10'

OPEN TO BELOW

BEDROOM No.4
11'-10" x 12'-0"

DECK

BREAKFAST
10'-10" x 7'-0"

KITCHEN
14'-0" x 13'-4"

UP

GREAT ROOM
17'-2" x 19'-2"

GUEST ROOM
12'-6" x 12'-0"

Width 60'-0"
Depth 47'-6"

LAUNDRY
10'-2" x 5'-8"

DN

STORAGE

TWO-CAR GARAGE
21'-4" x 21'-4"

DINING ROOM
11'-0" x

FOYER
11'-10" x 17'-0"

LIVING ROOM
14'-0" x 13'-6"

UP

STOOP

TO ORDER CONSTRUCTION DRAWINGS FOR THIS HOME SEE PAGES 248-255

BROOKSHIRE MANOR

DESIGN BY FRANK BETZ ASSOCIATES, INC.

Easy Living

Traditional, casual, elegant and comfortable describe this Southern Plantation style, with plenty of comfort zones and space for entertaining.

Designed to capture the romance and ambiance of the Southern low-country manors, this extraordinary home fits modern everyday life just fine, with lots of space for family gatherings and well-defined rooms for planned events. High-pitched gables and a wraparound porch provide a grand introduction, while Southern tradition flavors a unique interior, designed to take on whatever the owners schedule requires—even if it's just a little rest and relaxation. Throughout the home, fine arti-

STREET OF DREAMS
Brookshire Manor

Tomato red boldly accents a warm palette in the parlor—a great place for quiet conversation.

sanship and the architectural details of times gone by mixes what is ultra-comfortable with the utterly sophisticated.

Open formal rooms flank the foyer. The dining room is enhanced with an English antique cherry "dresser," a stunning complement to the tall windows and decorative columns that help define this space. Beyond the staircase, a formal parlor is crowned with a coffered ceilng. Nearby, a thoughtfully placed powder room is convenient for guests. The best views in the house are provided by the bay window in the grand room. Guests will linger in front of the massive fireplace before dinner, while family members will curl up with a good book.

A functional home office or guest suite to the rear of the plan has its own full bath. French doors open the area to a private covered porch that wraps around the house. The family wing provides a hearth room, warmed by a fireplace and natural light from a wall of windows. A well-planned kitchen features a center food-prep island, walk-in pantry and a wrapping counter that overlooks the breakfast nook.

This home, as shown in the photographs, may differ from the actual blueprints. For more detailed information, please check the floor plans carefully.

The spacious owners suite is tailored yet romantic in browns, neutrals, silks and velvet, with a splash of apple green.

A hand-painted armoire enhances the owners bedroom, while the architectural details of times gone by offer sophisticated style. This dashing suite offers five discrete areas: a retreat or sitting area, sleeping area, dressing space, bath and closet storage. Just steps away, a large family exercise gym with a juice bar invites early-morning workouts. A nearby secondary bedroom has its own full bath and a walk-in closet. This room allows accommodations for a guest, yet could easily be converted to an owners study. A bal-

Opposite: The grand room boasts a bowed window and an exquisite fireplace with a handcarved surround.

A step-up whirlpool tub and stunning arch-top window highlight the owners bath.

cony hall leads to two family bedrooms, each of which has a private bath. The lower floor includes a home theater and game room. Future space can be developed as the need arises. A service entrance leads to a laundry room, home office and side entry.

DESIGNER: © Frank Betz
Associates, Inc.
BUILDER: George Jenkins
& Associates
TERIOR DESIGN: Angela Cain Interiors
PHOTOGRAPHS: © Visual Solutions Co.

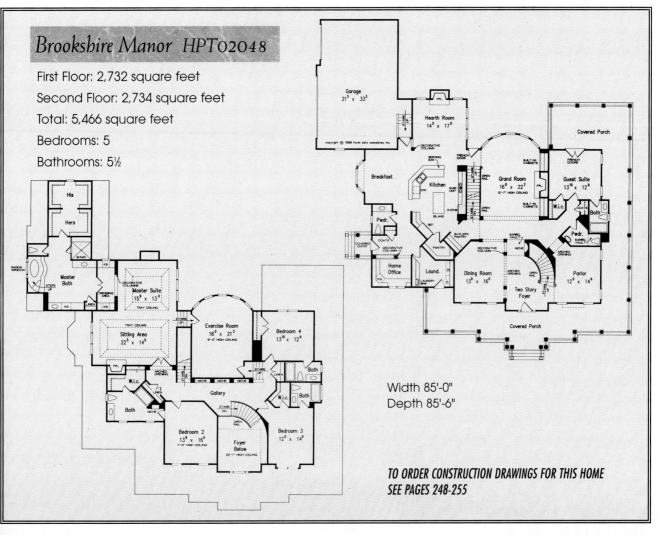

Brookshire Manor HPT02048

First Floor: 2,732 square feet

Second Floor: 2,734 square feet

Total: 5,466 square feet

Bedrooms: 5

Bathrooms: 5½

Width 85'-0"
Depth 85'-6"

TO ORDER CONSTRUCTION DRAWINGS FOR THIS HOME SEE PAGES 248-255

THE SUMMIT

DESIGN BY ALAN MASCORD DESIGN ASSOCIATES, INC.

Craftsman Classic

Rafter tails, gabled rooflines and charming transoms present an Arts and Crafts home that offers four bedrooms and plenty of soul.

This splendid version of Craftsman style is well suited to any neighborhood—be it an Arcadian suburb, uptown district or the heart of the country. The front covered porch, complete with built-in benches, opens to a grand foyer. Defined by crafted columns, this elaborate space provides a coat closet and a wide bench framed by cabinets. French doors lead to a private study, which features a window seat, built-in bookshelves and a plate shelf that surrounds the room. A fireplace will warm cool

STREET OF DREAMS
The Summit

Plenty of transoms and a fireplace with a tile surround add charm to the study.

evenings and cozy gatherings, while plenty of windows and a French door to a secluded deck provide natural light.

The foyer opens to a formal dining room through a banquet of decorative columns. This elegant space has a beam ceiling and a built-in hutch with recessed lighting, enhanced by a stunning triple window that brings in daylight or starlight. Just steps away from a 21st-Century kitchen, the dining room will easily serve traditional dinners as well as casual meals.

A spacious, well-planned kitchen is rich with wood cabinetry and hardwood floors. A work island is crowned by a hanging pan rack that's both decorative and useful. A built-in planning desk complements wrapping counter space and plenty of drawers and cabinets. The family cook will appreciate the walk-in pantry, vegetable sink and six-range stovetop. A double-sink counter overlooks a bright breakfast nook that's surrounded by views. French doors lead to an open porch and to a spacious sun room.

The nearby two-story great room boasts a massive stone fireplace, floor-to-ceiling windows and built-in bookshelves. Lovely French doors lead outside, extending the living space and inviting guests to enjoy the gentle breezes of a summer evening. Hardwood floors, recessed lighting and ten-foot ceilings enhance the entire first floor.

A beam ceiling crowns the formal dining room, which provides a built-in hutch.

Opposite: The family cook will love the central work island counter. A second counter with a double sink overlooks the morning nook.

The foyer provides a beautiful wooden bench. flanked by built-in curio cabinets.

Two staircases lead to the second floor, which offers a balcony overlook to the great room. Each of the two family bedrooms has a built-in bench or seat and plenty of wardrobe space. Compartmented lavatories provide each bedroom with a private entrance to the shared bath. A gallery hall with built-in shelves leads to a guest suite with a large wardrobe and triple window.

DESIGNER: © Alan Mascord Design Associates, Inc.
PHOTOGRAPHS: © Bob Greenspan (Interiors)
© David Papazian (Exterior)

This home, as shown in the photographs, may differ from the actual blueprints. For more detailed information, please check the floor plans carefully.

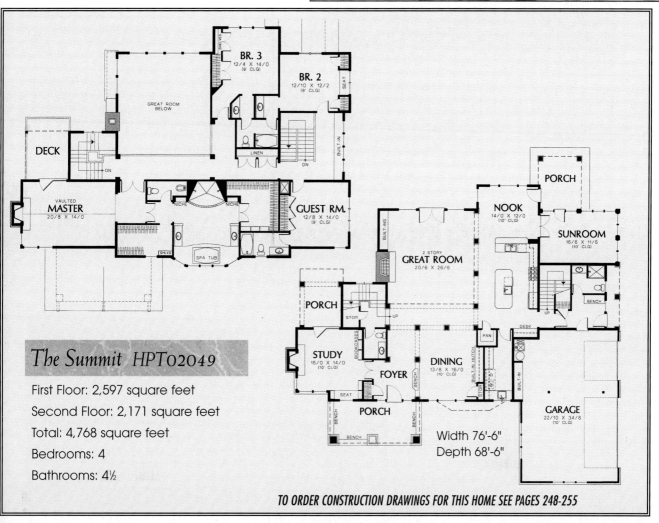

The Summit HPT02049

First Floor: 2,597 square feet

Second Floor: 2,171 square feet

Total: 4,768 square feet

Bedrooms: 4

Bathrooms: 4½

Width 76'-6"
Depth 68'-6"

TO ORDER CONSTRUCTION DRAWINGS FOR THIS HOME SEE PAGES 248-255

THE SCARBORO

DESIGN BY JOSEPH STARKMAN

Fine Art

With the spirit and enthusiasm of an artistic composition, this exceptional home uses natural, handcrafted materials and unique millwork to call up a fine sense of the past.

Traditional Craftsman architecture, cedar siding, brackets and battens introduce a home that blends the artisanship of simpler times with a fresh, thoroughly modern plan. Inside, exquisite details include wainscoting, chair rails and elegant paneling, which serve as the quintessential backdrop for mission-style furnishings. The side entry allows a see-through-the-house view of the golf course and leads to casual living space as well as the formal rooms.

STREET OF DREAMS
The Scarboro

Exquisite wainscoting, chair rails and handprinted reproduction wallcoverings create the perfect backdrop for mission-style furnishings in the formal dining room.

Above opposite: Lovely French doors open to a quiet study, which has built-in cabinets, a computer desk and a two-piece bath with a commode table vanity.

Below opposite: A vaulted ceiling crowns the great room, which features traditional built-ins and a sleek fireplace with a metal surround.

This home, as shown in the photographs, may differ from the actual blueprints. For more detailed information, please check the floor plans carefully.

The foyer opens to the formal dining room—an engaging blend of past and present, with handprinted reproduction William Morris wallcoverings and deep wall paneling. A pocket sliding door reveals the kitchen, as practical as it is beautiful. With oiled cherry wood upper cabinets and antiqued lower cabinets, this well-planned culinary paradise features up-to-date appliances, coffered ceilings, hand-painted tiles and cherry hardwood floors that continue in the dining room. Detailed millwork surrounds the passageway from the morning nook to the great room, which has a massive fireplace that shares its warmth with the entire area. The great room boasts a vaulted ceiling and provides built-in bookshelves on the fireplace wall.

THE SCARBORO

A study opens just off the foyer yet is close enough to the owners suite to provide a great workspace or even a home office. A nine-foot ceiling crowns the sophisticated décor of this stately, quiet room. Built-in cabinetry and a computer desk create a retreat for the homeowner but this stunning space can also serve as a parlor.

The central hall wraps around the study and leads to a laundry and a walk-in pantry. This area includes a powder room with hand-painted tortoise-shell walls and a furniture-style vanity console table. The laundry room provides a custom pullout drying rack and sewing table.

The lower-floor workshop and tiled plant-potting/gardener's area have direct stair access from the two-car garage. Nearby, a wine room with a gravel floor allows maintenance of proper moisture content in the room. A wrapping hall leads to the game room, which has a billiard table.

Wainscoting and a beverage rail surround the perimeter of the room. The adjacent media room has space for a large-screen television and full stereo center with surround sound. An artist's studio features a comfortable cork floor and Craftsman-inspired lighting fixtures.

DESIGNER: © Joseph Starkman,
Calgary, Alberta
BUILDER: Knightsbridge Homes Ltd.
INTERIOR DESIGN: Michelle Sigurdson, B.I.D.
Verve Interior Design
PHOTOGRAPHS: © Visual Solutions Co.

Rich furnishings add a touch of class to the powder room.

The great room overlooks the morning nook, which has a beam ceiling.

Custom millwork decks out the owners suite.

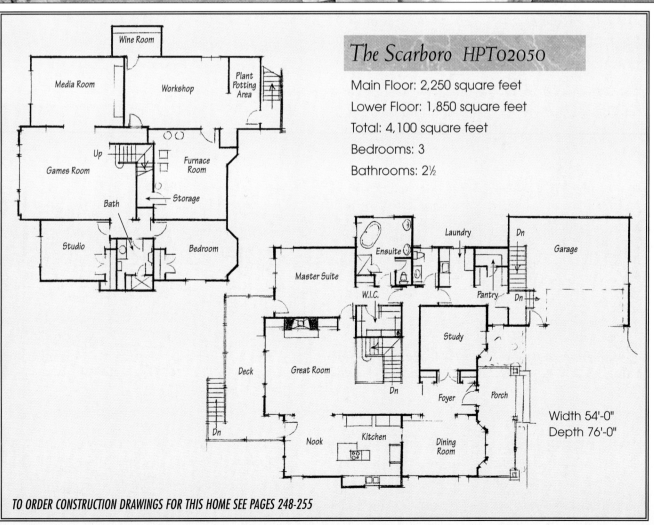

Wine Room

Media Room

Workshop

Plant Potting Area

Up

Games Room

Furnace Room

Bath

Storage

Studio

Bedroom

The Scarboro HPT02050

Main Floor: 2,250 square feet

Lower Floor: 1,850 square feet

Total: 4,100 square feet

Bedrooms: 3

Bathrooms: 2½

Laundry

Dn

Ensuite

Garage

Master Suite

W.I.C.

Pantry

Dn

Study

Deck

Great Room

Dn

Foyer

Porch

Width 54'-0"

Depth 76'-0"

Dn

Nook

Kitchen

Dining Room

TO ORDER CONSTRUCTION DRAWINGS FOR THIS HOME SEE PAGES 248-255

WHEN YOU'RE READY TO ORDER...

Let us show you our blueprint package.

Our Blueprint Package has nearly everything you'll need to get the job done right, with help from an architect, designer, builder or subcontractors. Each set of drawings is the result of many hours of work by licensed architects or professional designers.

QUALITY

Hundreds of hours of painstaking effort have gone into the development of your construction drawings. Each home has been quality-checked by professionals to ensure accuracy and buildability.

VALUE

Because we sell in volume, you can buy professional-quality construction drawings at a fraction of their development cost. With our plans, your dream home design costs only a few hundred dollars, not the thousands of dollars that custom architects charge.

SERVICE

Once you've chosen your favorite home plan, you'll receive fast, efficient service whether you choose to mail or fax your order to us or call us toll free at 1-800-521-6797. **For customer service call toll free 1-888-690-1116.**

SATISFACTION

Over 50 years of service to satisfied home plan buyers provide us unparalleled experience and knowledge in producing quality blueprints. What this means to you is satisfaction with our product and performance.

ORDER TOLL FREE
1-800-521-6797

After you've looked over our Blueprint Package and Important Extras on the following pages, simply mail the order form on page 255 or call toll free on our Order Hotline: 1-800-521-6797. We're ready and eager to serve you.

For customer service, call toll free 1-888-690-1116.

THE BLUEPRINT PACKAGE

Each set of construction drawings is a related gathering of plans, diagrams, measurements, details and specifications that precisely show how your new residence will come together. Each home design receives careful attention and planning from our expert staff to ensure quality and buildability. Sets may include:

Frontal Sheet

The artist's sketch of the full exterior of the house provides a projected view of how the home will look when built and landscaped. Large ink-line floor plans show all levels of the house and offer an overview of your new home's livability.

SAMPLE PACKAGE

Foundation Plan
This sheet shows the foundation layout including support walls, excavated and unexcavated areas, if any, and foundation notes.

Detailed Floor Plans
These sheets show the layout of each floor of the house. Rooms and interior spaces are carefully dimensioned and keys are given for cross-section details provided later in the plans. The positions of electrical outlets and switches are shown.

House Cross-Sections
Large-scale views show sections or cut-aways of the foundation, interior walls, exterior walls, floors, stairways and roof details. Additional cross-sections may show important changes in floor, ceiling or roof heights of the relationship of one level to another. Extremely valuable for construction, these sections show exactly how the various parts of the house fit together.

Interior Elevations
Many of our drawings show the design and placement of kitchen and bathroom cabinets, laundry areas, fireplaces, bookcases and other built-ins. Little "extras," such as mantelpiece and wainscoting drawings, plus moulding sections, provide details that give your home a custom touch.

Exterior Elevations
These drawings show the front, rear and sides of your house and give necessary notes on exterior materials and finishes. Particular attention is given to cornice detail, brick and stone accents or other finish items that make your home unique.

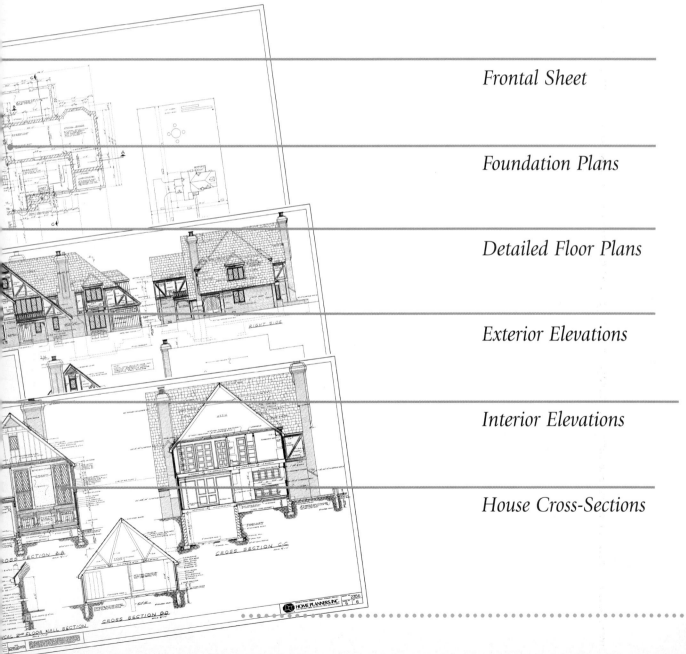

Frontal Sheet

Foundation Plans

Detailed Floor Plans

Exterior Elevations

Interior Elevations

House Cross-Sections

Important Extras To Do The Job Right!

Introducing eight important planning and construction aids developed by our professionals to help you succeed in your home-building project.

MATERIALS LIST

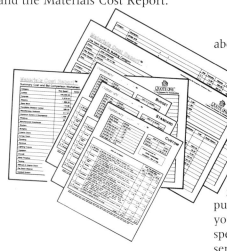

(Note: Because of the diversity of local building codes, our Materials List does not include mechanical materials.)

For many of the designs in our portfolio, we offer a customized materials take-off that is invaluable in planning and estimating the cost of your new home. This Materials List outlines the quantity, type and size of materials needed to build your house (with the exception of mechanical system items). Included are framing lumber, windows and doors, kitchen and bath cabinetry, rough and finish hardware, and much more. This handy list helps you or your builder cost out materials and serves as a reference sheet when you're compiling bids. A Materials List cannot be ordered before construction drawings are ordered.

SPECIFICATION OUTLINE

This valuable 16-page document is critical to building your house correctly. Designed to be filled in by you or your builder, this book lists 166 stages or items crucial to the building process. It provides a comprehensive review of the construction process and helps in choosing materials. When combined with the construction drawings, a signed contract, and a schedule, it becomes a legal document and record for the building of your home.

QUOTE ONE®

Summary Cost Report / Materials Cost Report

A new service for estimating the cost of building select designs, the Quote One® system is available in two separate stages: The Summary Cost Report and the Materials Cost Report.

The Summary Cost Report is the first stage in the package and shows the total cost per square foot for your chosen home in your zip-code area and then breaks that cost down into various categories showing the costs for building materials, labor and installation. The total cost for the report (which includes three grades: Budget, Standard and Custom) is just $29.95 for one home, and additionals are only $14.95. These reports allow you to evaluate your building budget and compare the costs of building a variety of homes in your area.

Make even more informed decisions about your home-building project with the second phase of our package, our Materials Cost Report. This tool is invaluable in planning and estimating the cost of your new home. The material and installation (labor and equipment) cost is shown for each of over 1,000 line items provided in the Materials List (Standard grade), which is included when you purchase this estimating tool. It allows you to determine building costs for your specific zip-code area and for your chosen home design. Space is allowed for additional estimates from contractors and subcontractors. This invaluable tool is available for a price of $130 which includes a Materials List. A Materials Cost Report cannot be ordered before construction drawings are ordered.

The Quote One® program is continually updated with new plans. If you are interested in a plan that is not indicated as Quote One®, please call and ask our sales reps. They will be happy to verify the status for you. To order these invaluable reports, use the order form on page 255 or call 1-800-521-6797.

DETAIL SETS

Each set is an excellent tool that will add to your understanding of these technical subjects and help you deal more confidently with subcontractors.

PLAN A HOME®

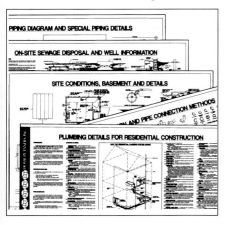

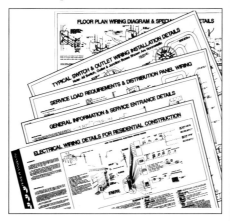

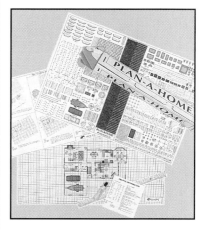

PLUMBING

If you want to know more about the complete plumbing system, these 24x36-inch detail sheets will prove very useful. Prepared to meet requirements of the National Plumbing Code, these six fact-filled sheets give general information on pipe schedules, fittings, sump-pump details, water-softener hookups, septic system details and much more. Color-coded sheets include a glossary of terms.

ELECTRICAL

Prepared to meet requirements of the National Electrical Code, these comprehensive 24x36-inch drawings come packed with helpful information, including wire sizing, switch-installation schematics, cable-routing details, appliance wattage, doorbell hookups, typical service panel circuitry and much more. Six sheets are bound together and color-coded for easy reference.

Plan-A-Home® is an easy-to-use tool that helps you design a new home, arrange furniture in a new or existing home, or plan a remodeling project. Each package contains:

- **More than 700 reusable peel-off planning symbols** on a self-stick vinyl sheet including walls, windows, doors, all types of furniture, kitchen components, bath fixtures and many more.

- **A reusable, transparent, ¼-inch scale planning grid** that matches the scale of actual working drawings (¼-inch equals one foot). This grid provides the basis for house layouts of up to 140 x 92 feet.

- **Tracing paper** and a protective sheet for copying or transferring your completed plan.

- **A felt-tip pen,** with water-soluble ink that wipes away.

Plan-A-Home® lets you lay out areas as large as a 7,500 square foot, six-bedroom, seven-bath house.

CONSTRUCTION

To help you understand how your house will be built—and offer additional techniques—this set of drawings depicts the materials and methods used to build foundations, fireplaces, walls, floors and roofs. Where appropriate, the drawings show acceptable alternatives. These six sheets will answer questions for the advanced do-it-yourselfer or home planner.

MECHANICAL

This package will help you make informed decisions and communicate with subcontractors about heating and cooling systems. The close up 24x36-inch drawings contain instructions and samples that allow you to make simple load calculations and preliminary sizing and costing analysis. Covered are today's most commonly used systems from heat pumps to solar fuel systems. The package is full of illustrations and diagrams to help you visualize components and how they relate to one another.

To Order, Call Toll Free 1-800-521-6797

To add these important extras to your set of construction drawings, indicate your choices on the order form on page 255 or call us toll free at 1-800-521-6797 and we'll tell you more about these exciting products. For customer service, call toll free 1-888-690-1116.

House Plans Price Schedule

One-set
Building Package

One set of vellum construction drawings
plus one set of study blueprints @ $.50 / square foot

Additional Set of Identical Blueprints in same order ....$50 set
(must be ordered within 60 days of original purchase)
Specification Outline ....$10 each
Materials List ....$ 70 each
(available only for those plans marked with a ✓)

All prices are subject to change without notice and subject to availability.

Purchase Policy

Accurate construction-cost estimates should come from your builder after review of the construction drawings. Your purchase includes a license to use the plans to construct one single-family residence. You may not use this design to build a second or derivative work, or construct multiple dwellings without purchasing another set of drawings or paying additional design fees. An additional identical set of the same plan in the same order may be purchased within a 60-day period at $50 per set, plus shipping and sales tax. After 60 days, re-orders are treated as new orders.

Sepias, vellums and other reproducibles are not refundable, returnable or exchangeable. Reproducible vellums are granted with a non-exclusive license to do the following:

❑ to modify the drawings for use in the construction of a
single home.
❑ to make up to twelve (12) copies of the plans for use in the
construction of a single home.
❑ to construct one and only one home based on the plans, either
in the original form or as modified by you.

Plans were designed to meet the requirements of the local building codes in the jurisdiction for which they were drawn. Because codes are subject to various changes and interpretations, the purchaser is responsible for compliance with all local building codes, ordinances, site conditions, subdivision restrictions and structural elements by having their builder review the plans to ensure compliance. We strongly recommend that an engineer in your area review your plans before you apply for a permit or actual construction begins. We authorize the use of our drawings on the express condition that you strictly comply with all local building codes, zoning requirements and other applicable laws, regulations, ordinances and requirements.

Index

To use the Index below, refer to the design name listed in alphabetical order (a helpful page reference and plan number are also given). To Order: Fill in and send the order form on page 255 or, if you prefer, fax to 1-800-224-6699 or 520-544-3086 or call toll free 1-800-521-6797 or 520-297-8200.

Before You Order...

Before filling out the coupon at the right or calling us on our Toll-Free Order Hotline, you may want to learn more about our services and products. Here's some information you will find helpful.

Quick Turnaround
We process and ship every order from our office within two business days. Because of this quick turnaround, we won't send a formal notice acknowledging receipt of your order.

Our Exchange Policy
Sepias, vellums and other reproducibles are not refundable, returnable or exchangeable. Since construction drawings are printed in response to your order, we cannot honor requests for refunds.

Revising, Modifying and Customizing Plans
The wide variety of designs available in this publication allows you to select ideas and concepts for a home to fit your building site and match your family's needs, wants and budget. Like many home-owners who buy these plans, you and your builder, architect or engineer may want to make changes to them. Your builder may make some minor changes, but we recommend that a licensed architect or engineer make most changes. As set forth below, we cannot assume any responsibility for construction drawings that have been changed, whether by you, your builder or by professionals selected by you or referred to you by us, because such individuals are outside our supervision and control.

Architectural and Engineering Seals
Some cities and states are now requiring that a licensed architect or engineer review and "seal" a blueprint or construction drawing and officially approve it prior to construction due to concerns over energy costs, safety and other factors. Prior to application for a building permit or the start of actual construction, we strongly advise you to consult your local building official who can tell you if such a review is required.

Local Building Codes and Zoning Requirements
Each plan was designed to meet the requirements of the local building codes in the jurisdiction for which they were drawn. Because building codes change from time to time and are subject to various interpretations, plans may not comply with any such code at the time they are sold to a customer. In addition, building officials may not accept these plans as final construction documents of record as the plans may need to be modified and additional drawings and details added to suit local conditions and requirements. We strongly advise purchasers to consult a licensed architect or engineer and their local building official before starting any construction related to these plans or applying for any permit. Your plan may need to be modified to comply with local requirements regarding snow loads, energy codes, soil and seismic conditions and a wide range of other matters. In addition, you may need to obtain permits or inspections from local governments before and in the course of construction. The purchaser is responsible for compliance with all the local building codes, ordinances, site conditions, subdivision restrictions and structural elements by having a licensed architect or engineer review the plans to ensure compliance. We authorize the use of our drawings on the express condition that you strictly comply with all local building codes, zoning requirements and other applicable laws, regulations, ordinances and requirements. **Notice: Plans for homes to be built in Nevada must be re-drawn by a Nevada-registered professional. Consult your building official for more information on this subject.**

Foundation and Exterior Wall Changes
Most of our plans are drawn with a basement foundation. Most professional contractors and builders can easily adapt your plans to alternate foundation types.

Disclaimer
We have put substantial care and effort into the creation of our construction drawings. However, because we cannot provide on-site consultation, supervision and control over actual construction, and because of the great variance in local building requirements, building practices and soil, seismic, weather and other conditions, WE CANNOT MAKE ANY WARRANTY, EXPRESS OR IMPLIED, WITH RESPECT TO THE CONTENT OR USE OF OUR CONSTRUCTION DRAWINGS OR BLUEPRINTS, INCLUDING BUT NOT LIMITED TO ANY WARRANTY OF MERCHANTABILITY OR OF FITNESS FOR A PARTICULAR PURPOSE.

Terms and Conditions
These designs are protected under the terms of United States Copyright Law and may not be copied or reproduced in any way, by any means, unless you have purchased sepias or reproducibles which clearly indicate your right to copy or reproduce. We authorize the use of your chosen design as an aid in the construction of one single family home only. You may not use this design to build a second or multiple dwellings without purchasing another set of drawings or paying additional design fees.

Have You Seen Our Newest Designs?

Home Planners is one of the country's most active home design firms, creating nearly 100 new plans each year. At least 50 of our latest creations are featured in each edition of our New Design Portfolio. You may have received a copy with your latest purchase by mail. If not, or if you purchased this book from a local retailer, just return the coupon below for your FREE copy. Make sure you consider the very latest of what Home Planners has to offer.

Yes! Please send my FREE copy of your latest New Design Portfolio.

Offer good to U.S. shipping address only.

Name _____

Address _____

City _____ State _____ Zip _____

HOME PLANNERS, LLC
Wholly owned by Hanley-Wood, LLC
3275 WEST INA ROAD, SUITE 110
TUCSON, ARIZONA 85741

Order Form Key

HPT02

Toll Free 1-800-521-6797

Regular Office Hours:
8:00 a.m. to 8:00 p.m. Eastern Time, Monday through Friday
Our staff will gladly answer any questions during regular office hours. Our answering service can place orders after hours or on weekends.

If we receive your order by 4:00 p.m. Eastern Time, Monday through Friday, we'll process it and ship within 48 hours. When ordering by phone, please have your charge card ready. We'll also ask you for the Order Form Key Number at the bottom of the coupon.

By FAX: Copy the Order Form on the next page and send it on our FAX line:
1-800-224-6699 or 1-520-544-3086.

Canadian Customers
Order Toll-Free 1-877-223-6389

For faster service and plans that are modified for building in Canada, customers may now call in orders directly to our Canadian supplier of plans and charge the purchase to a credit card. Or you may complete the order form at right, adding the current exchange rate to all prices, and mail in Canadian funds to:

Home Planners Canada   301-611 Alexander Street
C/o Select Home Designs   Vancouver, BC, Canada
                                   V6A 1E1

OR: copy the Order Form on page 255 and send it via our FAX line:
1-800-224-6699.

The Home Customizer Kit®

"This house is perfect…if only the family room were two feet wider." Sound familiar? In response to the numerous requests for this type of modification, Home Planners has developed The Home Customizer® Kit. This exclusive kit offers our top-of-the-line materials to help make it easy for anyone, anywhere to customize any Home Planners design to fit their needs.

Some of the changes you can make to our plans include:

- Exterior elevation changes
- Kitchen and bath modifications
- Roof, wall and foundation changes
- Room additions and more!

The Home Customizer® Kit includes:

- Instruction book with examples
- Architectural scale and clear work film
- Erasable red marker and removable correction tape
- ¼"-scale furniture cutouts

The price of the Home Customizer® Kit is $50. The kit will give you the flexibility to have your changes and modifications made by our referral network or by the professional of your choice. Now it's even easier and more affordable to have the custom home you've always wanted.

ORDER TOLL FREE!
For information about any of our services or to order call
1-800-521-6797 or
520-297-8200
Browse our website:
www.homeplanners.com

SEPIAS, VELLUMS AND OTHER REPRODUCIBLES ARE NOT REFUNDABLE, RETURNABLE OR EXCHANGEABLE.

For Customer Service, call toll free 1-888-690-1116

HOME PLANNERS, LLC
Wholly owned by Hanley-Wood, LLC
3275 WEST INA ROAD, SUITE 110
TUCSON, ARIZONA 85741

THE BASIC PACKAGE
Rush me the following (Please refer to the Plans Index & Price Schedule on pages 252-253):
One-Set Building Package for Plan Number(s)@ $.50/sq. ft._____. $_____
___ Additional Identical Blueprints in same order @$50 per set $_____

ADDITIONAL PRODUCTS
Rush me the following:
___ Plan-A-Home® @ $29.95 ea. $_____
___ Specification Outline @ $10 each. $_____
___ Materials List @ $70 each. $_____
___ Home Customizer Kit @ $50 each. $_____
___ Detail Sets @$14.95 each; any two for $22.95; any three
    for $29.95; all four for $39.95 (Save $19.85). $_____
    ___Plumbing___Electrical___Construction___Mechanical
    (These helpful details provide general construction advice and
    are not specific to any single plan.)
___ Quote One® Summary Cost Report @$29.95 for 1; $14.95; for each
    additional, for plans_____ $_____
    Building location: City_____ Zip Code_____
___ Quote One® Materials Cost Report @$130 for plans_____ $_____
    (Must be purchased with original set of construction drawings.)
    Building location: City_____ Zip Code_____

POSTAGE AND HANDLING	1-3 sets	4 or more sets
Signature is required for all deliveries.		
Delivery: (No COD's)		
(Requires street address—No P.O. Boxes)		
• Regular Service (Allow 7-10 business days delivery)	$20.00	$25.00
• Priority (Allow 4-5 business days delivery)	$25.00	$35.00
• Express (Allow 3 business days delivery)	$35.00	$45.00

OVERSEAS DELIVERY: Fax, phone or mail for quote.

NOTE: All delivery times are from date Construction Drawings are shipped.

POSTAGE (From box above) $_____
SUB-TOTAL $_____
SALES TAX (AZ, MI & WA residents
       please add appropriate state & local sales tax.) $_____
TOTAL (Sub-total and Tax) $_____

YOUR ADDRESS (Please print)
Name _____
Street _____
City_____State_____Zip_____
Daytime telephone number (_____) _____

FOR CREDIT CARD ORDERS ONLY
Please fill in the information below:
Credit card number _____
Exp. Date: Month/Year _____
Check one ❒ Visa   ❒ MasterCard   ❒ Discover   ❒ American Express

Signature _____
Please check appropriate box: ❒ Licensed Builder-Contractor
               ❒ Homeowner

Order Form Key

HPT02

STREET OF DREAMS®

Street of Dreams, Inc. is a Washington-State-based private company that specializes in the production of trademarked luxury housing shows. Each show includes up to ten fully furnished custom homes situated on a single street within a premier subdivision and runs for five weeks, drawing an average of 50,000 attendees. The company has completed 55 events in 20 United States cities and three Canadian provinces, attracting more than three million visitors.

Well established as the most popular luxury home tours in North America, Street of Dreams® shows have earned a reputation for displaying the most innovative trends in residential architecture, interior design and furnishings, products and construction. The events stimulate lot values and home sales within the host community and generate new business for all of the participants. Developers, builders, interior designers and other industry professionals interested in participating in an upcoming Street of Dreams® event are encouraged to visit www.streetofdreams.com or contact Bryan Ashbaugh, CEO, at 425-483-0253.

Design by James E. Gilgenbach, Architect
Photograph by © Visual Solutions Co.

Top: Design by Lucia Custom Home Designers, Inc.
Photograph © Everett & Soulé